GODLY
SEXUALITY

GODLY SEXUALITY

a study of morality and marriage
Matthew 5:27-32

STEPHEN MANLEY

Cross Style Press

GODLY SEXUALITY
© 2018 by Stephen Manley

Published by Cross Style Press
Lebanon, Tennessee
CrossStyle.org

Edited by Delphine Manley

ISBN-10: 0-9987265-2-4
ISBN-13: 978-0-9987265-2-6

Printed in the United States of America.

CrossStyle.org

CONTENTS

MORALITY
THE FULFILLMENT OF THE KINGDOM

Spiritual Adultery (Matthew 5:27-30)   9
What a Link! (Matthew 5:27-30)   19
Just a Look (Matthew 5:28)   31
Looking at a Woman (Matthew 5:28)   41
Sexuality and Priority (Matthew 5:28)   51
In His Heart (Matthew 5:28)   61
Essentiality: Severity (Matthew 5:29-30)   71
Essentiality: Stumbling (Matthew 5:29-30)   81
Essentiality: Spiritual Priority (Matthew 5:29-30)   91
Proposition of Eternity (Matthew 5:29-30)   101
Places of Eternity (Matthew 5:29-30)   111
Physical Eternity (Matthew 5:29-30)   121
Place of the Effects (Matthew 5:29-30)   131
Punishment of the Effect (Matthew 5:29-30)   141
Progression of the Effect (Matthew 5:29-30)   151

MARRIAGE
THE FULFILLMENT OF THE KINGDOM

The Divorce Issue (Matthew 5:31-32)   163
Kingdom Marriage (Matthew 5:31-32)   173
The Main Subject (Matthew 5:31-32)   183
Spiritual Separation (Matthew 5:31-32)   193

MORALITY

THE FULFILLMENT OF THE KINGDOM

1

SPIRITUAL ADULTERY

MATTHEW 5:27-30

"You have heard that it was said to those of old, 'You shall not commit adultery.' But I say to you that whoever looks at a woman to lust for her has already committed adultery with her in his heart. If your right eye causes you to sin, pluck it out and cast it from you; for it is more profitable for you that one of your members perish than for your whole body to be cast into hell. And if your right hand causes you to sin, cut it off and cast it from you; for it is more profitable for you that one of your members perish, than for your whole body to be cast into hell" (Matthew 5: 27-30).

I come to this passage with fear and trembling. My heart has no condemnation or judgment toward anyone joining me in the study. Jesus' grace is sufficient for all, despite our past or marital status. The depth of God's grace is astounding. We all stand guilty in the truth of this passage. All men and women have lusted and been unfaithful in their heart's response if not in their physical action. Often we say everyone is guilty; it is for self-justification. The teenager cries, "Everyone is doing it!" Guilt loves company. Although we admit that everyone is guilty of lust in the heart, we must never make light of it. The purpose of acknowledging our guilt is a simple reality; only by the power of Jesus are we able maintain sexual purity.

The results of sexual lust are devastating and can cause a negative view of sex. Sexual perversions are many in number and variety, thus creating a view of all sex as sin. The Bible does not take this position. Wanting to trap Jesus in a controversy of divorce, the Pharisees asked, *"Is it lawful for a man to divorce his wife for just any reason?"* Without hesitation Jesus examined them with their Scriptures, proposing the standard of God's heart for sex. *"Have you not read that He who made them at the beginning 'made them male and female,' and said, 'For this reason a man shall leave his father and mother and be joined to his wife, and the two shall become one flesh.' So then, they are no longer two but one flesh. Therefore what God has joined together, let not man separate"* (Matthew 19:4-6).

In quoting this Scripture, Jesus gives the origin of sexual intimacy, an expression of God's nature. Because we are created in God's image, and the sexual drive is a part of us, this drive expresses the passion for intimacy in God's heart. This intimate union of a husband and wife supersedes the relationship with father and mother. The power of this intimacy results in *"one flesh."* We find nothing negative or shameful in these statements. Jesus calls us His bride, expressing His relationship with us as Christians. This imagery contains all sexual involvements and ramifications; therefore, we embrace our sexuality in the beauty of God's nature.

The devil has never created anything. He has never brought something out of nothing. He is a created being who attached himself to God's creation, using it for his own ends. Every sin is a perversion of something wonderful that God created. At the heart of every sin is a virtue, something right and good. This is the issue Matthew presents in our passage. If adultery were the problem, those of old would be justified. The issue is the passion of God's heart expressed in relationships but especially in the first male to female relationship, sexuality.

There is a contrast between the approach of those of old and Jesus' approach. Those of old were worried about the physical activity of adultery. Sexuality in their lives became an animal drive to control and limit. Marriage became glorified prostitution, justifying the satisfaction of selfish desires. Sexual expression, whether on the level of flirting, emotional involvement, or physical expression, must come from intimacy with Jesus. This is the life of a person merged with Jesus, expressing His nature and demonstrating His image.

SEVERITY

PROCLAIMED IN THE OLD TESTAMENT

Anyone studying the requirements of the law of God in the Old Testament is not surprised by the severity of Jesus' approach. In Leviticus God proclaimed the law for Israel, and more importantly the penalties for breaking the law. Concerning adultery, God told Moses, *"The man who commits adultery with another man's wife, he who commits adultery with his neighbor's wife, the adulterer and the adulteress, shall surely be put to death"* (Leviticus 20:10). God gave the same instructions in Deuteronomy: *"If a man is found lying with a woman married to a husband, then both of them shall die — the man that lay with the woman, and the woman; so you shall put away the evil from Israel"* (Deuteronomy 22:22).

These statements are severe. God is serious about sexual purity, the seventh commandment in the Ten Commandments. Through the progression of time into Jesus' day, the severity lessened. The scribes and Pharisees brought to Jesus a woman who had been caught in the act of adultery. They proclaimed Moses' instructions to stone anyone found in this woman's situation (John 8:1-11). The accusers applied this only to the woman, but where was the man? These men had so justified themselves that they were excused from the law concerning adultery.

PROGRESSED INTO THE NEW TESTAMENT

Jesus gave us the New Covenant understanding of sexual purity. The writers of the epistles said it repeatedly. Paul proposed, *"For this is the will of God, your sanctification: that you should abstain from sexual immorality; that each of you should know how to possess his own vessel in sanctification and honor, not in passion of lust, like the Gentiles who do not know God; that no one should take advantage of and defraud his brother in this matter, because the Lord is the avenger of all such, as we also forewarned you and testified. For God did not call us to uncleanness, but in holiness. Therefore he who rejects this does not reject man, but God, who has also given us His Holy Spirit"* (1 Thessalonians 4:3-9). This statement is so powerful that it deserves a study dedicated to its content. Do not allow the passion of lust to dominate your body. The dominance of your body is the right only of the Holy Spirit. He is the One merged with you. Live in His purity. If you do not allow the Holy Spirit dominance of your body, you are rejecting God not man! God must inhabit your sexual expressions.

We must hear the cry of the Scriptures. *"Do you not know that the unrighteous will not inherit the kingdom of God? Do not be deceived. Neither fornicators, nor idolaters, nor adulterers, nor homosexuals, nor sodomites, nor thieves, nor covetous, nor drunkards, nor revilers, nor extortioners will inherit the kingdom of God"* (1 Corinthians 6:9-10). Contained in this list of ten sins, four relate to sexuality. The writer of the Book of Hebrews said, *"Marriage is honorable among all, and the bed undefiled; but fornicators and adulterers God will judge"* (Hebrews 13:4). We can only conclude from this that your sexuality is important to God, and it is tied to His presence in you. Do not violate it!

PROPOSED IN OUR PASSAGE

As we view the various problems involved in oneness with Jesus, sexuality comes boldly to the front. Although all areas are important and may vary in importance to different people, sexuality leads the parade. The overall divisions of the material in our passage reveal the truth (Matthew 5:27-30). The opening verse reflects on the traditional view of *"those of old"* (Matthew 5:27), mentioned once and contained in one verse. Then Jesus gives His view, which is equated with the view of the Scriptures, and thus the view of God's heart. However, it is only one verse in length (Matthew 5:28). The next two verses give us the bulk of the material (Matthew 5:29-30). These bold statements call for radical action and leave an imprint on the reader. This is serious!

"Those of old" focused on the physical act of adultery, while Jesus focused on the lust of the heart. Whether a physical act or a fantasy of the heart does not make a difference in severity. There is never just a physical act of adultery. There may be a fantasy of the heart without the physical act, but there is never a physical act without the fantasy. The problem is the severity of the involvement. Jesus does not advocate the removal of the body parts involved in the sexual act. He speaks about the *"eye"* and the *"right hand."* We will discuss these body parts in additional studies. Jesus suggests these things as the avenue to the fantasy. Although the physical act was severe in the Old Testament, the lust of the heart is most important in the New Covenant. This condition matters!

Everything we have talked about thus far involves our eternal destiny. Our eternal destiny is not about good people compared to bad people, or moral compared to immoral. Family, raising children, and the proper role of the husband and wife are not highlighted here. Jesus ended this section of His discourse with the subject of *"hell."* Your sexuality controls your eternal destiny because it expresses "who you are" not "what you do." The call of God is not that you abstain from specific physical activities but that you embrace His nature through the framework of your masculinity or femininity.

14

SPIRITUALITY

PROCLAIMED BY PAUL

The Scriptures equate physical sexuality with spirituality in a realm unexplainable yet consistently highlighted. Paul applied oneness with Jesus as being filled with the Holy Spirit, calling everyone to submit to this union. Practically applied, submitting to God is submitting to one another. He started with, *"Wives, submit to your own husbands, as to the Lord"* (Ephesians 5:22). A wife's submission to her husband is not because she is submitted to God, but in her daily walk as she submits to her husband in the physical, she is submitting to God in the spiritual.

Husbands are not in a superior position because they are to submit to their wives as Christ submitted to the Church. Practically applied, this submission is to be, *"Just as Christ also loved the church and gave Himself for her, that He might sanctify and cleanse her with the washing of water by the word"* (Ephesians 5:25-26). In fact, *"Husbands ought to love their own wives as their own bodies; he who loves his wife loves himself"* (Ephesians 5:28). Think of the oneness and unity expressed in these statements! The sexualities of the husband and wife are merged until they are one. Paul then quotes God saying, *"For this reason a man shall leave his father and mother and be joined to his wife, and the two shall become one flesh"* (Ephesians 5:31).

What is the fabric of this oneness? Paul said, *"This is a great mystery, but I speak concerning Christ and the church"* (Ephesians 5:32). The joining of the husband and wife in their sexuality is a mystery like the joining of Jesus and His Church, the believer. Paul does not give an example of oneness, or oneness in marriage as an example of the oneness of Jesus' Spirit merging with the believer. The sexuality of marriage engages the spiritual world in its oneness! This concept explains the belief that marriage is not complete unless God is involved. Marriage is not a simple union between two physical beings, but it is a spiritual union between God, the bride, and the bridegroom. Sexual intercourse is not a physical act but an encounter with the unseen spiritual world.

Those who have experienced spiritual warfare realize this reality. A study of the cities of pagan worship in the New Testament epistles reveals this truth. These pagan centers involved sexual activities because they believed the sexual ecstasy they had with temple prostitutes created a better union with their god. In the world of spiritual warfare, it is well known that the best way to pass demons from one person to another is through sexual intercourse. In the sexual union, the two people involved touch the spiritual reality of the other. Can you imagine what God intended in marriage? No wonder Paul called this intimate connection a mystery.

Now read carefully the words of Paul to the Church of Corinth. *"Do you not know that your bodies are members of Christ? Shall I then take the members of Christ and make them members of a harlot? Certainly not! Or do you not know that he who is joined to a harlot is one body with her? For 'the two,' He says, 'shall become one flesh.' But he who is joined to the Lord is one spirit with Him"* (1 Corinthians 6:15-17). The Greek word "kollao," translated *"is joined,"* means "to glue" or "to weld." The language Paul used for sexual oneness is the language used for oneness with Jesus. What a mystery!

PARALLEL IN THE SCRIPTURES

God used the Old Testament prophets to accuse Israel of being a harlot. The prophecy of Hosea is based on this imagery. God selected Hosea. Over several years God trained Hosea in the school of practical ministry. Hosea married a prostitute, they began a family, and she led Hosea through years of heartache involving betrayal and unfaithfulness. Hosea experienced through his sexual union the same unfaithfulness that God was having with Israel. This experience enabled Hosea to stand before Israel and tearfully speak the words of God. *"My people ask counsel from their wooden idols, and their staff informs them. For the spirit of harlotry has caused them to stray, and they have played the harlot against their God"* (Hosea 4:12). This language is repeated often throughout the Old Testament.

John wrote, *"Then one of the seven angels who had the seven bowls filled with the seven last plagues came to me and talked with me, saying, 'Come, I will show you the bride, the Lamb's wife'"* (Revelation 21:9). Jesus used this imagery in parables (Matthew 22:1-14; 25:1-13). He did not give physical illustrations to express spiritual realities but to show the connection between the sexuality of husband and wife and the spiritual realm of oneness with Jesus.

PATTERN OF JESUS

Jesus brings us to this thought in our passage. He establishes a pattern in these illustrations. He did not come to destroy the Scriptures (Matthew 5:17). The opposite happened in Jesus' life. The Trinity God placed His nature in our world as a Book, the Scriptures, describing the core of God! Jesus, the Second Member of the Trinity, set aside all He had as God to become one of us. As a human being, Jesus was filled with the Holy Spirit, God's nature. Then Jesus stepped into the Scriptures, the nature of God, in submission to being shaped in His living. The nature of God in His being and in written form produced the life of Jesus. He fulfilled every jot and tittle of the Scriptures.

He was unusual for the Old Covenant hour but not for the New Covenant day. The righteousness of the New Covenant people will exceed the righteousness of the best of the Old Covenant, the scribes and the Pharisees (Matthew 5:20). If they did not live up to the potential of the Old, they could never match the righteousness of the New! To illustrate this Jesus said murder in the physical realm is now equated with hate in the spiritual realm (Matthew 5:21-26). Hate is spiritual murder, as real as physical death created by a physical man.

If this is true of murder, how much more it must be true with adultery (Matthew 5:27-30). Lust in the spiritual realm is spiritual adultery; it is as certain as the physical adultery created by lust. We are to be filled with the Spirit of Jesus, embrace His Word, and let His nature mold our inner and outward lives to show who He is. Our sexuality must be determined by His nature not by our body drives. This determination is not a call to sexual purity but to intimacy with Jesus. How often have we played the role of the harlot in the spiritual realm of our lives? We will know sexual purity only by our union with His nature!

2

WHAT A LINK!

MATTHEW 5:27-30

"You have heard that it was said to those of old, 'You shall not commit adultery.' But I say to you that whoever looks at a woman to lust for her has already committed adultery with her in his heart. If your right eye causes you to sin, pluck it out and cast it from you; for it is more profitable for you that one of your members perish than for your whole body to be cast into hell. And if your right hand causes you to sin, cut it off and cast it from you; for it is more profitable for you that one of your members perish, than for your whole body to be cast into hell" (Matthew 5: 27-30).

The Gospels of Luke and Mark give various parts of the Sermon on the Mount, leading some to conclude that the Sermon on the Mount is a variety of spiritual messages spoken by Jesus throughout His ministry. Matthew does not do this in his Gospel account. He shows a consistency in the message from the Beatitudes to the closing story with Jesus systematically declaring the content of the Kingdom of God.

The Beatitudes are the beginning and the foundation of Jesus' truth. In all otherworld religions there is a journey where you earn, merit, and discipline your life to progress to your goal. What these religions insist that you accomplish Jesus gives! In Christianity we are in a state of poverty, absolute helplessness in our spirit (Matthew 5:3). We are to embrace this helplessness with grief until it becomes the attitude of our lives (Matthew 5:4). In this state we are filled with His Spirit (Matthew 5:5), uniting His resource with our helplessness and forming a new creature called the Kingdom of Heaven. Meekness, fullness, mercy, purity, peace, and rejoicing flow through us in this intimacy. In this state of being, we become salt and light (Matthew 5:13-16), and it is not what we do, but who we are in Jesus.

This proposal is a radical idea, different from all other proposals. You might think it contrary to the Scriptures, the Law, or the Prophets. Jesus clarified His position regarding the Scriptures (Matthew 5:17-20). He did not come to destroy the Law or the Prophets but to fulfill. The Scriptures are the nature of the Trinity God in our world, not ancient creed or laws for living, and it is the desire of God's nature in written form. The Second Member of the Trinity became man filled with the Holy Spirit, God's nature. This Man filled with God's nature stepped into the Scriptures in submission. The Holy Spirit, the inner nature of God, and the Scriptures, the outward nature of God, shaped His life. He was the prototype of the New Covenant person, and He demonstrated God's nature. All Kingdom people are to be like Him, exhibiting a righteousness exceeding anything anyone has ever known, even the scribes and Pharisees (Matthew 5:20).

Jesus gave six illustrations of His proposition (Matthew 5:21-48). The first is "murder" (Matthew 5:21-26). Murder is in the physical realm while hate and anger are in the spiritual, which is spiritual murder. The contrast is between *"You have heard that it was said to those of old"* and *"But I say to you."* Those of old taught a self-centered adjustment of the Scriptures. The Holy Spirit, God's nature, speaks the truth of the Scriptures (the nature of God in written form). The Living Word and the Written Word communicate truth! Abstaining from a physical act is not the cry of God's heart; we must be indwelt with God's nature.

Jesus' second illustration is "morality;" however, there is a link between His first (Matthew 5:21-16) and second (Matthew 5:27-30) illustrations.

PARTNERSHIP

These two illustrations have a "partnership." This partnership is between the inner being of man and the unseen spiritual world. Although this partnership is not the complete picture, it is the beginning of the idea we need to comprehend. According to the Old Testament, the creation of man's structure was a dichotomy. *"And the Lord God formed man of the dust of the ground, and breathed into his nostrils the breath of life; and man became a living being"* (Genesis 2:7). The *"dust of the ground"* constitutes the physical body of man. In other words, God formed the physical body of man from what was already created, but the inner being of man came from the inner being of God when He breathed into man His life. When God united with man in this way He created "a living being," uniting the inner being of man with his physical being.

The inner being of man is man's link with God's heart, the spiritual world. That link is why physical acts can never produce spiritual life. Mere physical existence is only death, and religious ceremonies carried out in the physical can never produce spiritual life. God made the inner being of man in His image, and only that inner being can link with God's nature. *"But the natural* (physical) *man does not receive the things of the Spirit of God, for they are foolishness to him; nor can he know them, because they are spiritually discerned. But he who is spiritual judges all things, yet he himself is rightly judged by no one"* (1 Corinthians 2:14-15). The *"natural man"* is a person without the link of his inner being with the Spirit of God. He is spiritually dead.

We enter death through sin. The spiritual link that allows us to live in the resource of God's nature is broken. We live out of our flesh, satisfying the comfort and catering to the desires of the flesh. This life produces a religion sourced by the strength of the flesh, causing *"those of old"* to cry, *"You shall not murder"* (Matthew 5:21). They considered this a high standard, and although it was to be applauded and honored, it was difficult to carry out in the flesh. Man's control and discipline of his physical urges is the best he can accomplish in his flesh. From the physical view, these urges are acceptable but need limited expression.

What if man could again know the spiritual link in his physical life? Can he be born from above (John 3:3)? Can God breathe into my flesh the breath of His nature, reestablishing the link? If God's nature produces my life, will He not establish a new level of living? God's nature is love, and this love is the standard of the spiritual realm. All the feelings of anger, hurt, and jealously will be replaced with love, concern, and empathy. I will no longer need to control and manage my physical desires because God's nature in me changes those desires. My flesh cannot produce this change, and my discipline cannot source it. This change happens when the Spirit of God breathes in me!

Jesus was filled with God's nature, the Holy Spirit, making Him the prototype of this link. He submitted to God's nature in the Scriptures. The nature of God in Jesus and the nature of God in written form shaped His physical life. Thus, you can experience forgiveness from Jesus. He sources what is best for you with no agenda for Himself. He died on a cross, giving you the gift of salvation that you cannot earn, and establishing the spiritual link between you and Him.

Let me give you another illustration of this link between you and Jesus. If this link is reestablished, what will happen in your sexuality? *"Those of old"* could not conceive of victory in their sexuality beyond controlling their physical acts. *"You shall not commit adultery"* (Matthew 5:27) was a high standard for any person sourced by his flesh. The sexual body drive is natural, but they viewed it like their hunger drive or their need for sleep. Why should this sex drive, a natural part of man's physical life, not be satisfied? They saw it as a physical appetite with no significant ramifications.

"Those of old" thought Jesus' words, *"that whoever looks at a woman to lust for her has already committed adultery with her in his heart"* was an overbearing standard. How could this be? Abstaining from the physical expression of the sex drive was difficult to maintain, so

how could Jesus expect anyone to control his or her thoughts as well? If He advocated purity in a person's thoughts, He would need to change the sex drive. The body craves what it craves! But Jesus spoke from the perspective of a Spirit filled New Covenant man! What if a link with the spiritual world could change the focus of our sexuality? Jesus did not want to remove the sex drive, but He proposed a refocusing of this drive in our lives!

If we are filled with God's nature, and our being is properly linked with the spiritual world, can Jesus' suggestion be a reality? Can a person's sexuality not be focused on selfish satisfaction? Can we view the opposite sex through the eyes of Jesus? If we are radically changed within, then there is no need for self-control of our sexual desires. Can the nature of God merge with me in every area of my life including my sexuality, producing His image in me? This merge between God's nature and me is the acceptable righteousness of the New Covenant!

PRODUCTION

We now need to investigate the rest of this idea. When the inner being of man links with the spiritual, this link acts on the physical. Man's inner being produces the physical expressions, and we must not be confused on this issue. When the inner being of man links with God's heart (the spiritual), this link determines man's physical expression. When a person is not linked with God's heart, he or she suffers the consequence of spiritual death, but we must not see them as nonexistent. The inner being of man does not disappear, but he or she is separated from all that God intended and enters destruction.

When the inner being does not merge with God's nature, that man's surrender is to self-satisfaction, ultimately destroying his being. When man does not allow God to source his physical life, that man resorts to the demonic nature of self-centeredness. All thoughts and attitudes become selfish. Even when his actions appear to be generous, those actions are driven by selfish motives, and all relationships are fostered and maintained in selfishness. There is no righteousness in man; all our righteous acts are filthy rags (Isaiah 64:6). We become a product of self, taking God's place in our inner being.

Even the best of *"those of old"* could not imagine why Jesus would say, *"You shall not murder"* (Matthew 5:21). Are there no limits to the expression of one's self-centeredness? The prevenient grace of God does not leave us at the mercy of our own selfishness. Do we not have enough decency in the inner being to limit our evil expressions? The attitudes of hate, jealously, hurt, and revenge spring from the inner being left to "self." Without God's nature, "self" is the source of the physical activity.

Jesus said, *"But I say to you that whoever is angry with his brother shall be in danger of the judgment"* (Matthew 5:22). How can anyone who knows the state of humanity advocate such a proposal? A person might curb his or her physical action and resist murder, but the idea of not getting angry or hating is ludicrous. I cannot help the way I feel. No one understands me. I only hate people who deserve it because they are mean, vile, and hateful people who do terrible things to make me uncomfortable. I will not kill them, but I should at least be allowed to hate them!

Can the inner being of man link with the Spirit of

God, allowing that Spirit to control his physical life? Can I be filled with God's nature? Can God's nature saturate my life like a liquid fills a sponge? God's nature cannot be limited to the religious sections of my inner man, expressing that religion on occasion. God's nature must control and saturate all areas of my life. Jesus calls for a new production in my life, determined by our inner link.

"Those of old" advocated the standard that, *"You shall not commit adultery"* (Matthew 5:27) with pride. But can we expect any less from those possessed by their physical drive, controlled by a selfish inner being, living for pleasure, comfort, and self-gratification? Under this scenario the sex drive naturally becomes an instrument for self-pleasure, developing all manner of perversions. There must be some restraint, thus we do not commit adultery! To restrain from committing adultery is the best the self-centered man can ever think or dream of achieving.

Jesus said, *"But I say to you that whoever looks at a woman to lust for her has already committed adultery with her in his heart"* (Matthew 5:28). This sounds impossible! How can a person maintain such a standard in a body with a powerful sex drive? No one can master his sexuality to that extent. But what if this expectation is not about you controlling, mastering, or disciplining your sexuality? Jesus promotes a New Covenant, God's nature filling the heart of man. If man merges with the Divine Heart of God, his physical drives will be produced by God's motives. This merging means death to the self-centered motives that fill our lives and control our physical drives. We are to see the person of the opposite sex as Jesus sees them. Our weakness is filled with His nature (Matthew 5:3). In this merge we become the Kingdom of God, a new creature. God's attitude of meekness, hungering for righteousness, mercy, purity of heart, peace, and joy fill our lives (Matthew 5:3-11). God now produces our perspective, even our sexuality.

PRESENTATION

We have one more fact that we want to highlight. The inner being of man linked with God's nature, acting on the physical world, reveals the content of the man's inner being. The linked man becomes an expression of his spiritual being. Our physical body was never intended to dictate or control our actions but is a platform to display the inner heart. The physical body is not useless or unimportant but is vital to mankind's eternal being.

Jesus is our example. In His flesh He is the visible image of the invisible Father. God's heart did not change because of Jesus. When we study the Old Testament, we are somewhat confused about the Trinity God's heart. What is He really like? Jesus clarifies this issue, and we must interpret the Old Testament revelation of God in light of Jesus, the complete revelation of God. As Jesus is this revelation He also shows us what we are to be, our destiny. Jesus was linked with God's nature in His inner being. This nature controlled and gave content to His physical life. Everything God's nature sourced through Jesus was purposed to bring us into the same relationship. Jesus was the prototype of who we are to be!

"Those of old" proposed the standard of, *"You shall not murder"* (Matthew 5:21). This standard was the best their inner hearts could produce, and it revealed the inward link

they had with the spiritual, which left them filled with self. They were responsible for fulfilling the law of God and sourced their own righteousness. Their physical lives were filled with expressions of hatred, jealousy, and judgment. The Pharisees were more concerned about proper activity on specific days rather than the welfare of a man with a withered hand (Matthew 12:9-14). Their lives were filled with hypocrisy. They adjusted the Scriptures by their interpretation to foster their lifestyles (Matthew 15:3-9). Their physical actions displayed this hypocrisy, and they acclaimed their relationship with God although they acted out this relationship with self.

Can a person merge with God's nature? Can our inner beings be filled with God's nature until we think as He thinks, see as He sees, and feel what He feels? Is that the purpose of Jesus' life? If we link with God's nature, that oneness produces Jesus' life in us, and we become the visible image of His nature. If Jesus possesses our inner being, we will express Him in our outward living. He cannot be hidden.

"Those of old" proposed, *"You shall not commit adultery"* (Matthew 5:23). Flirtations, emotional involvements, and lust were acceptable to them. After all, "who we are" is demonstrated in the acts of our flesh. We cannot help ourselves! We must curb and attempt to control our urges. But Jesus said, *"But I say to you that whoever looks at a woman to lust for her has already committed adultery with her in his heart"* (Matthew 5:28).

This statement is ridiculous unless certain things are true. God created our sexuality, a natural element of our being. There is nothing wrong with sexual desire. The difficulty is in who is directing and determining the quality of this sexuality. The inner being of a person will determine the physical expression of their sexuality. When self controls my inner being, the motive of selfishness dominates and displays my sexuality. My pleasure and satisfaction are paramount to me. My physical expressions will be shaped by what is acceptable in my culture, but will always be expressions of self-centeredness. I will use others for self-gratification. Can I be filled with the Spirit of God? Jesus proposed a New Covenant where the inner being is filled with God's nature. Can the Spirit of God possess my sexuality in redemptive power? Can my sexuality become the expression of my inner being filled with God's nature?

How can we know who is linked with our inner being? Our physical lives demonstrate that link! This is not an appeal to change your physical activity. We do not suggest a program for retraining your physical response to the stimuli of your physical world. Jesus calls us to link our inner being with His. He is our only hope!

3

JUST A LOOK

MATTHEW 5:28

"But I say to you that whoever looks at a woman to lust for her has already committed adultery with her in his heart" (Matthew 5: 28).

Our visual world is dominated and controlled by sexuality. Why use sexuality at the heart of our advertisements? Sexuality is what gets us to look, accept, and purchase. Sexuality influences and directs our fashion causing us to sacrifice comfort and convenience to appear sensual. Sexuality is about the visual; we must look! My wife watches the Food Channel on television. I walked in on a program where three pastry chefs were competing in a cake contest. The winning chef had created a beautiful, sleek display nearly five feet high where cake was formed into various objects resting on each other. The judges applauded the sensual appearance of the cake. Even our food is judged by sexuality.

Playboy published its first magazine in 1953, and today that publication is a 4.9 billion dollar business. The domain name (*sex.com*) is valued at 65 million dollars. 28,258 people view pornography every second. Every thirty-nine minutes, a new pornographic movie is produced. Christians are not exempt from these statistics. More than fifty-three percent of men attending Promise Keepers said they viewed pornography weekly. Forty-five percent of Christians admit pornography is a major problem in their home. "Looking" has taken over our lives!

The Scriptures place a significant focus on the "eye." In the Sermon on the Mount Jesus calls the eye, *"the lamp of the body."* He said, *"The Lamp of the body is the eye. If therefore your eye is good, your whole body will be full of light. But if your eye is bad, your whole body will be full of darkness. If therefore the light that is in you is darkness, how great is that darkness"* (Matthew 6:22-23). "Looking" becomes the entryway into our lives. When the perspective of looking has Jesus' nature, the being is filled with light, but when the perspective of looking is self-centered, darkness prevails.

The basis of the first temptation was the eye. The devil suggested to Eve that God did not tell the whole truth. *"So when the woman saw that the tree was good for food, that it was pleasant to the eyes, and a tree desirable to make one wise, she took of its fruit and ate"* (Genesis 3:6). But this was more than a temptation because the consequences of sin affected the "looking" of this couple. After Adam and Eve had eaten the fruit, *"then the eyes of both of them were opened, and they knew that they were naked; and they sewed fig leaves together and made themselves coverings"* (Genesis 3:7).

The miracles of healing the blind were highlighted signs of the Messiah. A person receiving their sight is never found in the Old Testament, and Jesus was the only one in the New Testament to heal blinded eyes. The opening of our eyes is a reality of the New Covenant. In the New Covenant, man's nature is transformed when Jesus removes blindness (false seeing) and gives sight (proper perspective).

The Greek language has only one word for hearing in the New Testament, which is "akouo," but there are five Greek words for "seeing." The Greek word "horao," translated "to look," conveys the idea to experience or perceive. The Greek word "optanomai" is rarely used and means "to be visible or to appear." "Theaomai" refers to a spectator or one who "beholds." "Theoreo" refers to a spectator at a religious festival. The Greek word in our passage is "blepo," translated *"looks,"* means "to see" with an emphasis on the function of the eye. This word is as the opposite of blindness. "Blepo" is the absolute for insight and used for intellectual or spiritual perception, appearing one hundred and thirty-seven times. Most of those uses are in the present tense introducing a state of continual action.

Jesus presented the idea of a relationship between the inner being of a person and their physical life. This idea was a part of the theological battle that raged between Jesus and the Pharisees. The Pharisees, committed to the letter of the law, were outraged with Jesus because He was committed to the Spirit of the law. Jesus' view was different because He was the first Spirit-filled person, the prototype of the New Covenant person living in the fullness of God's nature. Jesus submitted Himself to the Scriptures; the written form of God's nature, and His physical life was an expression of His intimacy with that nature. Although physical activity was present, it was never the determining factor of His actions. Everything physical happened because of the inner spiritual nature. This was the conflict between Jesus and the Pharisees.

The Pharisees were concerned with only physical appearance. They gave money generously only because they wanted to be seen by those watching (Matthew 6:1-4), and they prayed to impress those listening (Matthew 6:5-7). They fasted so others would be in awe of their sacrifice (Matthew 6:16-18). In their opinion, *"For they* (the disciples) *do not wash their hands when they eat bread"* (Matthew 15:2) was a transgression of the tradition of the elders. Their concern was a focus on the physical activity.

Jesus called everyone to have a righteousness that exceeded the righteousness of the scribes and Pharisees. No one *"will by no means enter the kingdom of heaven"* without that exceeding righteousness (Matthew 5:20). Jesus had a central theme with six illustrations in "The Fulfillment of the Kingdom, Application" (Matthew 5:21-48). In these illustrations he contrasted the Pharisees' satisfaction with physical achievements with the state of the inner being. *"Those of old"* were concerned with only murder. They had anger management classes to teach the discipline not to kill. But the New Covenant went far beyond this physical standard. Why be angry? Why not eliminate murder in the spiritual realm as well as the physical (Matthew 5:21-26)? Jesus proposed this idea about sexuality. Let us look at this closely.

DISREGARDED

"Those of old" proposed *"You shall not commit adultery"* (Matthew 5:27). Jesus said, *"But I say to you that whoever looks"* (Matthew 5:28). But *"those of old"* DISREGARDED physical sight. The highest state of righteousness they could conceive was abstinence from sexual involvement with another man's wife. They considered refraining from the physical act of sex as the only guideline for righteousness. Why was that? They lived a self-sourced religion and that was the best they could produce. When a person controlled his sexual body drive enough to maintain this self-imposed physical boundary, he was applauded.

But the righteousness of the New Covenant, the fullness of the Spirit, is not content with this level. Then Jesus introduced the idea of "*looks*"! Seeing is not a negative in the Scriptures. The writers of the Scriptures emphasized God's looking. In the Old Testament, God rejected Saul as king and informed Samuel of His plan to find a king among the sons of Jesse. Samuel was to take a heifer to Bethlehem to offer a sacrifice and invite Jesse and his sons. Samuel chose Jesse's son, Eliab, as the most likely candidate to be the new king. *"But the Lord said to Samuel, 'Do not look at his appearance or at his physical stature, because I have refused him. For the Lord does not see as man sees; for man looks at the outward appearance, but the Lord looks at the heart'"* (1 Samuel 16:7).

Hundreds of years later Jesus reminds the Jews of how God sees! The Jews have rejected the way God sees by disregarding the *"looks"* in our passage. They want a god who *"looks,"* measures and judges them by their physical acts. That kind of judgment is more comfortable to them than God probing the depth of their heart motive. They want a physical religion where they can parade their achievements, but Jesus focused on "*looks*."

God requires from us only what is in His life. Could Jesus' challenge be to see as God sees? Our passage is not an intensified rule about sexuality. The old law was, "*You shall not commit adultery*" (Matthew 5:27). Is the new rule to not "*look at a woman to lust for her*" (Matthew 5:28)? Jesus' call to the Kingdom person is not that of maintaining a new level of physical activity, but He proposes a change in our nature where He controls our perspective!

Jesus' call is not focused only on sexuality but is at the heart of every life area. We are to see all situations as Jesus sees them, think as Jesus thinks, and have the mind of Christ (Philippians 2:5). If Jesus sources us with the same nature God sourced Him, we will see, feel, and consider all things as He does! Our passage is not a call to control what we see but to allow Jesus to fill our weakness with His strength (Matthew 5:3-12). Our view will be determined by which nature is sourcing self, Spirit or us.

DOOR

We can expand this thought. Physical sight is a DOOR into our inner being's spiritual realm. In our verse, the link between "*looks*" and "*heart*" explodes with truth. The eye is the gateway into a person's heart. Some people think we can look into the eyes of a person and see his or her soul, and Jesus established this connection.

If the eyes are the gateway into a person's heart, then we can project the truth that what we see becomes food for the soul. Our eyes become the mouth of our soul, and we take in the supply of material that constructs our inner being. What the eye sees feeds the lust of the mind and produces adultery in the heart, which makes Jesus' statement in our verse obvious. The link between what the eye sees and what the heart produces is not minor. This link is the reason Jesus said, *"If your right eye causes you to sin, pluck it out and cast it from you"* (Matthew 5:29). This verse is Jesus' cry against the means that feeds the soul.

In biblical terms, the right eye is the strongest and gives visions into the distance. What if the right eye, designed to direct life toward the long range, the everlasting, becomes tricked? What if that eye becomes fixated on the present moment? Suddenly that person's life is thrust into immediate satisfaction, which is called pleasure. Instead of that soul being fed the building materials to construct a life worthy of eternity, that soul is fed the pleasures of destruction temporary and worthy only of damnation in hell.

DELIGHT

If the problem of the inner soul were contained in what we see, it would be a simple matter. Blind people would be the most spiritual among us, but blindness does not guarantee righteousness. Two people looking at the same object may perceive two different things. Therefore, we must advance to this idea: physical sight is the DELIGHT of the inner beings' spiritual realm, and our spiritual life determines what we see!

Now we want to look carefully at our verse. *"But I say to you that whoever looks at a woman to lust for her*

has already committed adultery with her in his heart" (Matthew 5: 28). In this statement Jesus gives a purpose clause saying, ***"that whoever looks at a woman to lust for her has already committed adultery with her in his heart."*** This statement is based on the authority of the Person who fulfills every aspect of the Scriptures (Matthew 5:17). Jesus, filled with God's nature, submitted His life to the shaping of God's nature in the written Scriptures, which gave Him the proper insight. The main verb of the purpose clause is the Greek word "moicheuo," translated **has committed adultery**. The Greek word "blepo," translated **looks**, is a participle (a verb acting as an adjective). The verb gives content to the subject, **whoever**. This English word is a translation of "pas ho," translated literally as "all the." Who is the "all the?" It is "the looking on a woman" ones. The problem Jesus presented is not contained in looking on a woman. The problem is for what purpose a person looks! If the purpose is to ***"lust for her"*** he ***"has already committed adultery with her in his heart."*** Jesus said the heart determines the motive, which controls the purpose for "looking." The problem is not in the "looking" but in the "heart."

Jesus again brings us back to the central issue of the Sermon on the Mount. Unless we embrace our spiritual poverty (Matthew 5:3-4) and are filled with His nature, we will continue to be sourced by our selfish, self-centered nature. The perspective of this nature sees everything for its own benefit and pleasure. This nature is the opposite of the cross style, the perspective of God. We were created in spiritual poverty, helplessness, to merge with God's nature. We were created to be dependent not independent.

Thus, our passage is not an intensified rule we are to

obey. *"Those of old"* established their rule, *"You shall not commit adultery"* (Matthew 5:27). Jesus did not make a new set of rules in the New Covenant. The Kingdom person and those self-sourced look at a woman from different agendas. Jesus wants us merged with His divine heart to see with His perspective, revealing we are in the New Covenant.

You and I can now understand! In the New Testament, there is not a new discipline to control my physical appetite or correct an animal drive in me. I do not need to be motivated to protect my manhood. I now see myself as God sees me through His heart. "Turning the other cheek" becomes a possibility (Matthew 5:39). "Going the second mile" becomes a standard practice in my life (Matthew 5:41). Living without hate and anger becomes the state of my existence (Matthew 5:22). The nature of God fills my life and produces a new "look"!

The disciples questioned Jesus when He began preaching in parables. He said, *"Because it has been given to you to know the mysteries of the kingdom of heaven, but to them it has not been given"* (Matthew 13:11). Those sourced by self could not understand the parables Jesus told. For instance, who can understand leaving ninety-nine sheep in the fold to risk your life for a stray sheep lost in a storm at midnight (Matthew 18:10-13)? Who can understand the payment plan of God's heart? Jesus told of workers hired at various times throughout the day, some with only one hour of work while others toiled for the entire day. At the close of that day the owner paid everyone the same wage (Matthew 20:1-16)! Does that make any sense? That payment plan makes sense only to those sourced by God's nature and see with His eyes.

Being filled with God's nature and seeing with His eyes is the cry of Jesus! Will you allow God to source your sexuality by His nature?

4

LOOKING AT A WOMAN

MATTHEW 5:28

"But I say to you that whoever looks at a woman to lust for her has already committed adultery with her in his heart" (Matthew 5: 28).

Jesus is brief in His presentation of our passage. He gives the view of *"those of old"* in one verse (Matthew 5:27), and in the next verse He states His opinion (Matthew 5:28). The Greek word "ego," translated *"I,"* appears only as an emphatic emphasis. The subject *"I"* is included at the ending of the verb *"say"*; therefore, *"ego"* is unnecessary except for forceful emphasis. Jesus proclaims His word above the authority of *"those of old."* He was the first to experience the Kingdom of Heaven, and He speaks from this platform. He does not add to or complement the Scriptures but points to what God intended in the Scriptures. *"Those of old"* missed the heart of God in the Scriptures.

Sexuality was a complicated problem in Jesus' day and remains so in our day. You would think we would have progressed further in our 2,000 years of learning. To correct this problem, Jesus could have exclusively focused on adultery, but He did not see that as the solution for His day or ours. He knew the root problem of sexuality was not adultery. If no one ever committed adultery again, it would not solve the problem of sexuality. The same was true with murder (Matthew 5:21-26). Murder is a symptom of anger. Jesus' Sermon on the Mount focused on our helplessness, which needs the resource of God's nature (Matthew 5:3). Our nature is perverted, and we need rebirthing. The perversion of our sexuality is only one expression of the problem, our nature.

Jesus clearly stated His intent when He said, *"But I say to you that whoever looks at a woman to lust for her has already committed adultery with her in his heart"* (Matthew 5: 28). A legalist approaches this problem by focusing on *"looks."* Is Jesus intensifying and increasing the rule for the New Covenant? The best the Old Covenant could conceive was, *"You shall not commit adultery"* (Matthew 5:27). In the New Covenant, the old rule is replaced with, "You shall not look on a woman." Jesus' proposal is not to solve the problem by raising our activity level; instead, He proposes we allow Him to make a radical change in our nature as He sources our activity.

A new rule would be a distraction from the New Covenant. The New Covenant problem is not sexual expression or the activity of "looking"! Jesus never condemned "looking." How can we exist a day in our world without looking at a person of another gender, knowing of their sexuality? When I look at another man

I know his masculinity, and when I look at a woman I know her femininity, recognizing and honoring who each is. Jesus gives no condemnation for "looking" because it is right.

The problem is in the rest of the verse, *"to lust for her,"* focusing on intent and motive. Jesus highlights what drives the "looking." Previously we have studied the role of sexuality in the fall of the human race. The Scriptures say that the moment Adam and Eve sinned, *"Then the eyes of both of them were opened"* (Genesis 3:7). This does not mean that they were blind before their sin. They were "looking" from the moment of their creation to their sin. Their "looking" was not their sin! But when they sinned, *"Then the eyes of both of them were opened, and they knew that they were naked; and they sewed fig leaves together and made themselves coverings"* (Genesis 3:7). The first recorded effect of their sin was their new view of their sexuality. God came walking in the garden in the cool of the day. Adam and Eve hid themselves (Genesis 3:8). When God found them, Adam confessed, *"I heard Your voice in the garden, and I was afraid because I was naked; and I hid myself"* (Genesis 3:10). God asked, *"Who told you that you were naked?"* (Genesis 3:11). Their view of sexuality was different. "Looking" was not the problem but the motive for the "looking" had become one. Their nature was not the same!

We must never perceive sin as merely a deed that needs forgiveness. It is easy to say, "I sinned; God forgives me. I did it again; God forgives me again." Although sin does need forgiveness, we need to open the door that deals with the nature of the sin that possesses us! The Scriptures repeatedly tell us that Jesus came to destroy the works of the devil (Hebrews 2:14; 1 John 3:8). We must never be content to be saved "in" our sin; we must be saved "from" our sin. Jesus died not to only forgive but also to deliver us from the nature of sin! He wants to deal with our sexuality.

PURPOSE

Let us examine the nature of man. What was altered in the perspective of man's nature when he sinned? It was a shift in PURPOSE! The picture of woman's creation is incredible, and the setting of woman's creation gives necessary information to the purpose. Who can know the mind of God? There are conclusions we can draw in the progression of the creation story. Adam was the crowning creation of God's endeavor. God created all living things with sexuality, weaving sexuality into the fiber of the nature both in plants and animals. He made all animals male and female. But this creation type was not true with Adam! There was no feminine complement to Adam as with all other creation.

"The Lord God planted a garden eastward in Eden, and there He put the man whom He had formed" (Genesis 2:8). Adam named all the animals. He enjoyed fellowship with God and all the goodness of the garden. God commanded Adam never to eat of the tree of the knowledge of good and evil (Genesis 2:17). It was his responsibility to tend and keep the garden (Genesis 2:15). We are never told how long he did this alone and without a counterpart. God had sexuality written into the creation of everything, but something was missing in Adam!

God recognized the problem and said, *"It is not good that man should be alone; I will make him a helper comparable to him"* (Genesis 2:18). She is a *"helper."* She is not the opposite but a complement, one who rushes to aid and fulfill. She is *"comparable to him,"* the same as he. She is not his subordinate, his servant, a tool for his pleasure, an instrument for use, or another of his objects among many. *"And the Lord God caused a deep sleep to fall on Adam, and he slept; and He took one of his ribs, and closed up the flesh in its place. Then the rib which the Lord God had taken from man He made into a woman, and He brought her to the man"* (Genesis 2:21-22). She completes man and is the final touch that makes up what is lacking in him.

Adam's response to God's gift was astounding. He said, *"This is now bone of my bones and flesh of my flesh; she shall be called Woman, because she was taken out of Man"* (Genesis 2:23).

The Hebrew word "etsem," translated *"bone,"* has the meaning of "substance or self." *"Bone of my bones"* can be translated "self of my self." Adam referred to this new aspect of his sexuality as *"Woman,"* and his reason for this title was, *"Because she was taken out of Man."* He was saying, "She is me!" This statement is a reference to God's intended relationship of sexuality, and the depth of this relationship is revealed in the following statement. *"Therefore a man shall leave his father and mother and be joined to his wife, and they shall become one flesh"* (Genesis 2:24). *"Therefore"* means that what has been spoken is the basis for what is going to be said. Based on the purpose and method of Eve's creation, a man and a woman will be joined (glued or welded) together as *"one flesh."* God's intent for creating woman was not to separate her from man! God never intended for male and female to be at odds, separated, or warring. His intent was that man and woman together are one! The purpose of her creation was a continuation of oneness.

There is a progression in the biblical statements. Woman was taken out of the body of man. Man breaks forth with a description of who she is. He proclaims, "She is me!" The biblical statement about marriage is, ***"Therefore a man shall leave his father and mother and be joined to his wife, and they shall become one flesh"*** (Genesis 2:24). God clearly defined this statement based on the method of woman's creation, the reaction of man to woman's creation, and the purpose of her creation. This is God's intent for marriage. Jesus reminded the Pharisees of God's purpose when they were arguing about divorce (Matthew 19:5). God made this statement in Genesis before there were *"father and mother"* to leave. He clearly stated His dream and purpose for the oneness to occur in sexuality.

Then Adam and Eve sinned, altering mankind's nature! How tragic! The sin was not a deed of sin that could be forgiven and forgotten. The nature affecting the "looking" of man was changed. They did not think in terms of unity, giving their lives to each other, but they became divided, using each other for personal benefit. Sexuality became self-serving, causing man and woman to be unglued, separated, and selfish, bringing the tragedy of divorce. Let us look again at our passage (Matthew 5:28). This passage is not Jesus' new commandment as the New Covenant approach to sexuality. He focused His attention on the problem in the nature of humanity. We do not "look" at each other correctly because our perspective comes from a changed nature. Jesus died to restore us to our previous condition, which is God's nature indwelling and filtering through our sexuality. He calls us to God's original plan of sexuality!

PERFORMANCE

We not only have a shift in "purpose," but also a shift in PERFORMANCE. Sexuality is never just physical activity. The physical realm was designed by God to be a platform for the demonstration of the spiritual nature of man. Although the essence of man cannot be judged by his physical deed, his physical deeds are a demonstration of who he is. We see this in relation to God! Paul declared that the physical creation of the world gave clear evidence of the *"invisible attributes"* of God (Romans 1:20). We can see His eternal power and Godhead plainly manifested in Jesus. The eternal Word, God, *"became flesh and dwelt among us, and we beheld His glory, the glory as of the only begotten of the Father, full of grace and truth"* (John 1:14). *"He is the image of the invisible God"* (Colossians 1:15).

"Those of old" were concerned only with the physical activities of their sexuality. They saw their sexuality as an animal drive isolated from their spiritual life. They needed to control and limit it within the boundaries of the proper physical activity of marriage. Jesus expressed a view far beyond controlling performance. He asked, "What is the expression of the spirit interacting with your flesh?" The sexual act of marriage gives physical expression to the oneness (glued or welded) that exists between man

and the one who is *"bone of my bones, flesh of my flesh."*

The physical expression of sexuality in biblical language (Greek) is "ginosko," translated "to know" (Matthew 1:25). This word is the strongest Greek word for intimacy, relationship, and oneness on the highest spiritual level. The expression of sexuality in the physical realm is the welding of two spiritual lives into one. All other expressions are a perverted demonstration of an inner soul focused on self. "Looking" is not the problem; Jesus did not propose a further physical regulation of restricted sight. His cry is for a heart change. Marriage has become a means to use our spouse for personal benefit and satisfaction instead of giving one's self to the other in oneness.

POSSESSION

Our passage is also a shift in POSSESSION. The Greek word "epithymeo," translated "lust," is the same Greek word translated "covet." *You shall not commit adultery"* is the seventh of the Ten Commandments. The tenth commandment is, *"You shall not covet your neighbor's house; you shall not covet your neighbor's wife, nor his male servant, nor his female servant, nor his ox, nor his donkey, nor anything that is your neighbor's"* (Exodus 20:17). The heart of the word is the idea of possession. If I covet or lust after my neighbor's house, I desire to take it from him, claim it as mine, and possess it for myself. If this desire is achieved in the physical realm, I remove the possession from my neighbor and take it for myself.

In this act, I become a thief! In the spiritual world,

I am stealing my neighbor's house. Now bring this truth to our passage. God intended for our sexuality to be intimate, share one flesh, and know another by giving one to the other. When my sexuality is driven by my sinful nature, I become a thief. In the spiritual, I carry out the action of King David of old (2 Samuel 11), stealing my neighbor's wife!

Additionally, in the spiritual I steal from the woman herself what is not rightfully mine. I rob from her what is not mine to possess. I do not give; I take. My self-centered nature becomes a cancer devouring others for my benefit. I am a spiritual thief.

Jesus did not give a new rule for the new Kingdom. He calls us to live His intention for our sexuality. God's plan is to fill our being with His nature. Our sexuality must be focused and purposed in Him. There is nothing wrong with "looking." The problem is in my heart. In my helplessness I am incapable of changing my heart. This is a call to be HIS!

5

SEXUALITY
AND PRIORITY

MATTHEW 5:28

"But I say to you that whoever looks at a woman to lust for her has already committed adultery with her in his heart" (Matthew 5: 28).

Jesus extends a startling contrast in our passage so vivid that we cannot miss it! *"Those of old"* interpreted God's law according to their self-achievements. They viewed their sexuality as "an isolated body drive" to be controlled within the boundaries of decency. If they kept their sexuality in the boundaries of marriage, any pleasure or satisfaction was acceptable. The contrast here is with the Spirit-filled life, *"But I say to you."* The New Covenant restored us to God's intention from the beginning. Our sexuality envelops our creation and purpose for life. The presence of God must permeate every aspect of sexuality from the heart's intention to the practical physical expression. Jesus makes an amazing contrast!

The rule of old was, *"You shall not commit adultery."* The Jews loved this terminology because it was always about *"you"* and never about "them." We see this philosophy expressed when they drug a woman caught in the act of adultery to the feet of Jesus. They believed they were justified in their action; they leaned back ready to throw stones, their self-righteousness leading them to put this woman to death. Let us look carefully at what Jesus said in our passage. *"But I say to you that whoever"* (Matthew 5:28). *"Whoever"* is a translation of the Greek word "pas ho." "Pas" means "all," and "ho" means "the." The "looking ones" fall into the category of lusting and are included with no adjustment, no excuse, or no compromise! This does not allow us to drag anyone into the arena of scrutiny. We all stand in the spotlight of examination by the New Covenant standard!

We stand face to face with the truth that "looking at a woman" is not the problem. We live with a continual awareness of sexuality. Sexuality is in every facet of our lives, present in every relationship, and interwoven in all we are. As the passage unfolds, the problem is PRIORITY. The priority of life becomes our sexuality. Although sexuality may contribute to every area of living, it was not to dominate us. The male's expressions of masculinity are seen in his approach to circumstances, the way he walks, and in his relationships to the females around him. However, when masculinity dictates the man's life, he has violated the standard of the New Covenant. He may not have broken the commandment of *"those of old,"* but he has violated the intent of the New Covenant, which is intimacy with Jesus!

We see this in the Garden of Eden. Adam was the

crowning creation of God, placed in the garden with a command. *"Of every tree of the garden you may freely eat; but of the tree of the knowledge of good and evil you shall not eat, for in the day that you eat of it you shall surely die"* (Genesis 2:16-17). Adam's only relationship was with God because Eve had not yet been created. After he had named all the animals and tended the garden for a while, God became aware that His man was not complete in his sexuality. He put Adam to sleep and created woman out of His man. One day the devil had a conversation with Eve. They discussed the commandment that Eve had heard from Adam. Adam must have been present for this conversation because Eve ate of the fruit and *"gave to her husband with her"* (Genesis 3:6). Regardless of what Eve's temptation might have been, sexuality was involved in Adam's temptation. He could not conceive of living without her, and Adam made a choice between God and Eve. He gave up the embrace and sacrificed the oneness he had with God for what he thought was oneness with Eve.

Adam's blindness was the tragedy. He did not realize that without oneness with God, he could not have oneness with Eve. When Adam separated from God there was a separation between male and female. You have to give this careful consideration! Man was created in the image of God, and the woman was created out of the man. When man separated from his oneness with God, his oneness with the female could not continue. It is only because Adam had oneness with God that he could have oneness with Eve, his flesh. Without oneness with God, their oneness with each other deteriorated to a self-satisfying use of each other, resulting in competition and jealousy. The masculine human, being the strongest, now dominates and abuses. The feminine human becomes a tool or instrument for the man's service and pleasure. God created sexuality to complete the man, but without God the destructive force of evil makes man incomplete. What has Adam done? He has chosen sexuality over God. The destruction of this priority entered his home, his life, his children, and his world. It was inevitable!

In our passage Jesus highlights PRIORITY. The problem is not "looking"; it is PRIORITY! There is still more for us to consider.

FOCUS

Sexuality is the focus of our day, capturing our children at much younger years than before. Ten percent of all thirteen-year-olds have had sex. Half of all teenagers have participated in sex by the time they enter the tenth grade. One out of every five teenage girls will become pregnant. Two-thirds of all young adults finishing high school are already sexually active. We are focused on our sexuality in advertisements, fashions, literature, movies, and even comedy. We are obsessed with our sexuality. Jesus declared this to be the problem in our passage. The problem is not about "looking"; it is about priority!

Listen to our passage again. *"But I say to you that whoever looks at a woman to lust for her has already committed adultery with her in his heart"* (Matthew 5:28). Included in this statement, Jesus speaks of looking *"at her,"* lusting *"for her,"* and committing adultery *"with her,"* as He highlights the priority of our sexuality. The Greek word "pros," translated *"at,"* is a preposition of direction. This word marks the direction toward or to which something moves or is directed. It carries the idea of "in order to," expressing purpose. Man looks at woman with a distinct perspective in mind. The priority of his life has now become the focus of his "looking." He is dominated by this focus in every aspect of his sexuality.

The Greek word "autos," translated *"for her,"* is a pronoun of "self" used as an intensive to emphasize, and sets the woman apart from everything else. "Autos" is used with a proper name as *"Herod himself"* (Mark 6:17). Jesus again uses "autos," translated *"with her,"* focusing everything on the woman. Each time he use "autos" He highlights "looking." Jesus points out that the intent and purpose of man's sexuality has changed in priority. Man no longer has the original nature God created him nature. His focus is altered!

Jesus is strong in His emphasis on priority. The problem is not in the "looking"; the problem is in the focus of the "looking" and is at the root of Christian experience. Our nature has radically changed from its intended focus. We focus on controlling our desires, relationships, and our physical acts have become depraved. Why do we think dirty jokes are humorous? What attracts us to pornography? We are never satisfied with a little, but our desires increase in degree and intensity. Why would *"those of old"* be satisfied with pushing their sexuality aside and look to a rule to control their physical acts? Our focus is wrong! Can Jesus become our focus?

FORCE

We might tend to think the "focus" of sexuality is proper because it is deeply ingrained in every aspect of our lives. What is wrong with that? No one ever suggested that our sexuality be removed or eliminated. The problem seems to be the "force" of our sexuality, and Jesus highlights this in our passage. The Greek word "blepo," translated *"looks,"* is a participle, a verb serving as an adjective modifying the subject of the main verb, *"has committed adultery."* *"Whoever"* is a translation of the Greek word "pas ho" meaning "all the," now modified by *"looks."* The subject becomes "all the looking ones." *"Looks"* is also in the present tense, and refers to the continuous process of looking. The problem of concern is not the incidental or involuntary glance but the intentional and repeated gazing, which is the "force" present in the "looking." The Greek word "epithumsai," translated *"lust,"* indicates a goal or an act that follows the "looking." *"Lust"* describes the force of the "looking" in terms of purpose. Sexuality becomes the dominating force in life dictating the purpose of "looking."

James uses strong language to describe the force of lust. He said that it was never God's purpose or in His nature to tempt man to sin (James 1:13). Temptation does not come from God but comes from deep in the nature of man. The force of man's sinful nature drives the desires and perspectives of man. James uses the Greek word "exelko," translated "to drag away." *"But each one is tempted when he is drawn away by his own desires and enticed"* (James 1:14). The sinful nature of man forcibly controls man's looking and drags him away in the act of lust. The sinful nature permeates the perspective that controls physical action. James says this in the terms of sexuality when He writes, *"Then, when desire has conceived, it gives birth to sin; and sin, when it is full-grown, brings forth death"* (James 1:15).

Man can never break the force of sin in his life by a simple decision. *"Those of old"* could see no other way to maintain righteousness because they viewed sexuality as an animal drive they could not control. Therefore, they set their boundary to be that of refraining from sexual involvement with their neighbor's wife. All other sexual control was impossible because of the force of this sinful nature. But the force is not in the sexuality. If it were, then we must eliminate sexuality, not redeem it. The force is in the evil self-centered nature that fills man. God created man to be dependent on His nature, and sinful man decided to be independent, depending only on his self-focus and allowing this nature to dominate his sexuality.

Man's sinful nature not only dominates his sexuality, but it dominates his emotions also. Jesus gave six illustrations beginning with "anger" (Matthew 5:21-26). The best *"those of old"* could do was to control their anger within the boundaries of not committing murder. No one can love in every situation and forgive everyone because of the force of the sinful nature. The answer to this problem is not in the elimination of our emotions but in the redemption of our emotions through allowing God to remove the self-focus of our nature. So it is with our sexuality!

Jesus proposes a change in our nature. He wants to restore us to God's nature, making us the Kingdom filled with His presence. This proposal is not a call to anger management or a challenge to sexual discipline. This call is to a nature change. The self-centered nature must die. Listen to the cry of Paul. *"I have been crucified with Christ; it is no longer I who live, but Christ lives in me; and the life which I now live in the flesh I live by faith in the Son of God, who loved me and gave Himself for me"* (Galatians 2:20).

If the problem is "priority," what is the force of the priority? This is not a new message; it is "self." Self-centeredness focuses on self and is energized by self to satisfy its selfish desires. Sexuality dominated by self (the sinful nature) drives us to use sexuality for self-benefit and self-pleasure. This nature destroys God's purpose and intent of sexuality. I must die to my selfish, self-centered, self-focus.

FINALITY

There is another aspect of the "priority" in the "finality" of Jesus' statement. Any person who is possessed by his self-centered nature is dragged to a forced focus of self-possessed sexuality, and *"has already committed adultery with her in his heart."* The Greek word "ede," translated "already," means "even now." What happened in the physical "looking" is present in the heart of the person.

We must understand the proper progression of "looking." "Looking" at a woman lustfully does not cause a man to commit adultery in his thoughts. "Looking" does not control the thoughts; however, thoughts control the "looking" but not the heart. The condition of the heart dictates the thoughts, which dictates to the "looking." When lust reaches the "looking," it already exists in the heart, which is the dwelling place of man's nature.

The message was the same in Jesus' first illustration

of anger and murder. *"You shall not murder"* was the priority of *"those of old."* The physical was the best their self-centered, self-sourced nature could conceive on its own. The emotions of anger, temper, and jealousy under self-sourcing must be curbed enough not to commit murder. Curbing emotions is the best self-centered man can do. But Jesus proposed a radical change in man's behavior. When the self-centeredness of man is changed, anger will not have to be controlled because it will cease to exist.

This progression is the same with adultery. Self-centeredness of the heart dominates the sexuality and focuses it on adultery. The thoughts of adultery control the "looking." The thoughts of adultery are controlled by sexuality under the dominance of self-centeredness. Jesus did not propose a removal of sexuality but a restoration of man's nature. This would change man's heart, changing his thoughts and his "looking"!

This restoration is the message of the Kingdom of Heaven. You and I are helpless (Matthew 5:3). We give the appearance of being strong and capable as we attempt to be sourced by our helplessness, yet our failures and brokenness testify to our weakness. Jesus calls us to embrace our helplessness (Matthew 5:4). We are not helpless because we have sinned; we are helpless because of the way God created us. The "Comforter" can invade us only when we embrace our helplessness (Matthew 5:4). This heart alteration changes our perspective; the change in our perspective changes our thoughts; the change in our thoughts changes our "looking." Jesus is our only chance!

6

IN HIS HEART

MATTHEW 5:28

"But I say to you that whoever looks at a woman to lust for her has already committed adultery with her in his heart" (Matthew 5: 28).

The Scriptures express the focus of God on the heart! Samuel, the prophet, was instructed by God to go to Bethlehem and offer a sacrifice. He was to invite Jesse and his sons to accompany him, because God was going to select a member of this family to be the new king of Israel. Samuel was impressed by one of Jesse's sons, Eliab, because of his stature and his leadership among men. But God said to Samuel, *"Do not look at his appearance or at his physical stature, because I have refused him. For the Lord does not see as man sees; for man looks at the outward appearance, but the Lord looks at the heart"* (1 Samuel 16:7). This verse should give you insight into the importance of the heart in the mind of God as well as the content of the heart.

Have you had a moment when you became aware of how wrong you were about something, and this awareness swept over your life? Have you felt the heaviness of guilt crush in on you making it difficult to breathe? King David had such a moment. He had always been able to justify, excuse, and avoid all sense of responsibility, but when Nathan, the prophet, told a story that revealed truth to David's heart everything changed (2 Samuel 12). David cried out to God, *"Create in me a clean heart, O God, and renew a steadfast spirit within me"* (Psalms 51:10). This was not a cry of David for God to remove a blemish on his face so he would look better, and it was not a cry for financial prosperity. David faced a deep-seated awareness of need in his life. This cry was nothing superficial; David was dealing with his inner heart.

The wisest man in the world of his day said, *"For as he thinks in his heart, so is he"* (Proverbs 23:7). There is something powerful about the heart as it reaches in to the essence of our lives and shapes us. Our inner being is not shaped by our physical existence; it is our inner being that sources our lives. What makes this heart so powerful? How can we ignore it for so long? How can our physical existence become so dominating that the heart diminishes in value and importance?

Paul could not have expressed it more clearly. *"If you confess with your mouth the Lord Jesus and believe in your heart that God has raised Him from the dead, you will be saved. For with the heart one believes unto righteousness, and with the mouth confession is made unto salvation"* (Romans 10:9-10). What is this heart that determines the salvation of our lives? Does this not tell us what must be our top priority? Should this not be the focus of our being? What about my heart?

Jesus gave six illustrations to secure the understanding of true Kingdom existence. His proposal was so radical that His listeners had to adjust it to fit their level of understanding. How can He move them from *"those of old"* to *"I say to you?"* These six illustrations are powerful and touch every area of life, clarifying what the Spirit of God produces in man's life.

The only illustration that mentions the heart is the one dealing with sexuality. Does that mean that sexuality is at the core of our existence? Is sexuality so intertwined in every area of life that we cannot dismiss it as a segment of life? Does sexuality have it roots in our heart? Sexuality gives expression to each area of life, dominating language, dress, physical expressions, emotional outbursts, affections, understanding, self, and mannerisms. Is it correct to say that *"looks"* and *"lust"* flow from the heart? The progression of "looking" is important in our passage (Matthew 5:28). A man does not look, lust, and then commit adultery in his heart. He has adultery in his heart, which causes the look of lust. Looking and lusting are expressions of the twisted, self-centered sexuality rooted in man's heart. To correct this condition a change at the heart of sexuality is demanded. Our sexuality is not evil, but the nature of the sexuality is perverted!

The Greek word "kardia," translated "heart," is familiar. *"For the life of the flesh is in the blood, and I have given it to you upon the altar to make atonement for your souls"* (Leviticus 17:11). Because blood comes from the heart and flows back to the heart, the heart is the core from which life comes, and it is the center of man's being. We need to investigate this heart idea as it applies to our passage.

CONCENTRATION

The heart always has a focus. We use phrases such as: "I love you with all my heart"; "Even though we are separated, you are in my heart"; "My heart's desire is..." The heart has become the symbol of Valentine's Day, cards shaped like a heart, candy hearts, and drawings of the heart. Love that focuses on an object is expressed as belonging to the heart.

Love's focus is one of the uses of the Greek word "kardia" in the Scriptures. We make statements that express the object of one's love as something held in the heart. Paul was open with the people of Corinth, crying to them, *"Open your hearts to us. We have wronged no one, we have corrupted no one, and we have cheated no one. I do not say this to condemn; for I have said before that you are in our hearts, to die together and to live together"* (2 Corinthians 7:2-3). He expressed love to these people because they were in his heart!

Paul had the same feelings for the people of Philippi, remembering their first contact as he shared the Gospel with them. He is grateful for their growth and progress in the faith, confident that God, who started this work in them, would complete it. He said, *"Just as it is right for me to think this of you all, because I have you in my heart, inasmuch as both in my chains and in the defense and confirmation of the gospel, you all are partakers with me of grace"* (Philippians 1:7).

The heart is the dwelling place of the most intimate and loved objects of our lives. My heart controls what I love and do not love. My heart determines the something or someone I will cherish in my life. Christianity is a "heart religion"! Jesus settled the Pharisees' argument about the greatest commandment by quoting the Old Testament. *"You shall love the Lord your God with all your heart, with all your soul, and with all your mind.' This is the first and great commandment. And the second is like it: 'You shall love your neighbor as yourself.' On these two commandments hang all the Law and the Prophets"* (Matthew 22:37-40).

We now have clear insight into our passage (Matthew 5:28). *"Those of old"* saw their sexuality as a body function they had to control, requiring a law, *"You shall not commit adultery."* This law was the acceptable boundary that allowed them to live in their sexuality. The New Covenant view of sexuality is an issue of the heart, because sexuality is a focus or object of the heart! Adultery happens when a man *"looks at a woman to lust for her."* To what *"woman"* does Jesus refer? It can be any woman. The woman is not the love object of the heart; rather, the "looking" man's sexuality is the love object. In other words, the focus or object of the heart is a person's sexuality.

Jesus said that God gave the essence of marriage in the Scriptures. *"Have you not read that He who made them at the beginning 'made them male and female,' and said, 'for this reason a man shall leave his father and mother and be joined to his wife, and the two shall become one flesh?'"* (Matthew 19:4-5). The object of man's heart is to be the "woman" (*wife*) not sexuality. Adultery lives in the heart where the pleasure of sexuality is the object. My illustration for this truth is a boy and girl alone in the moonlight. The boy whispers to the girl, "I love you, so come on!" What would happen if he told the truth? "I love me, so come on!" That line will not get him the desired results, so he lies. Perhaps we really do not know the truth of our hearts. If I really love you I will not risk, hurt, or use you for personal benefit. The object of the heart is not you, but I!

Regardless, the institution of marriage is not the solution to our passage. A husband's heart can worship his sexuality and legally use his wife as an instrument for his selfish pleasure. That is the reason Jesus' focus is not on the physical act of adultery but on the object of the heart's love. When my wife is the object of my heart, my sexuality becomes a beautiful expression of that love, and the intimacy of our "oneness" brings completeness. The heart cannot be satisfied when a person's sexuality is the object of his/her heart.

Our passage proposes a question. What is the object of your heart? Is it your sexuality? Or is your husband or your wife the object of your heart? And if you who are single think this does not apply to you, you are wrong! Jesus calls you His bride, and He is to be the object of your heart!

CONTEMPLATION

"Heart language" is a thing of the mind. When a person is moved by facts and truth, we say he is disturbed in his mind. When the mind comes to a new understanding of truth that truth upsets the thought pattern. When we file an event or activity in the back of our mind, we have "hidden it in our heart." We do not discuss it, but constantly think about it. What are the things you have hidden in your heart?

Mary and Joseph experienced many things with Jesus. The event of His birth saw an appearance of angels, shepherds gathering at the manger, and wise men coming from the East bearing expensive gifts. Their escape to Egypt must have been a frightening circumstance for this peasant couple. This escape was to protect Jesus from the hatred of King Herod. When Jesus was twelve years old, they unknowingly left him in Jerusalem as they traveled with friends toward home. When they discovered He was not with them, they frantically searched for three days in Jerusalem only to find Him in the temple. Luke wrote, *"Then He* (Jesus) *went down with them and came to Nazareth, and was subject to them, but His mother kept all these things in her heart"* (Luke 2:51). The Greek word "diatereo," translated "kept," comes from the root word meaning, "to guard or watch." Mary stored all these memories in her heart.

None of this knowledge is new to us. We consistently deal with events in the past that we have "stored up" in our hearts. Circumstances of our childhood, abuses experienced at the hands of others, ridicule by childhood friends, and personal failures haunt us in our hearts. These things are not light or superficial but lie at the core of our being.

Jesus relates our sexuality to our hearts. This relationship is not a surface issue that we can discard as minor. The color of your eyes is not hidden in your heart, never gives you life trauma, and is not tied to the core of your being because the color of your eyes is not a heart issue. Jesus says that our sexuality is extremely different because sexuality is a matter of the heart.

The approach used by *"those of old"* is not adequate. They considered sexuality a body drive to control. All they needed was an adequate rule to guide sexual activity. But

Jesus insisted that it was a heart issue. The need of my sexuality cannot be legislated, because it is hidden in the heart. Jesus did not propose eradication or the elimination of sexuality. His cry was for proper understanding and pondering of your sexuality on the heart level. If our response is to ask about the right way to think about sexuality, we find ourselves with another set of rules. Jesus described our sexuality as the core of our "helplessness" (Matthew 5:3). Our helplessness must be filled with His resource. If His resource fills our helplessness, it will radically affect what we keep in our hearts. The proper approach to this problem is not about doing right but about being right.

Let us not forget to note the progression of sexuality in our passage (Matthew 5:28). We do not look, lust, and then commit adultery in our hearts. Adultery is already "hidden in the heart," which produces looking and lusting. Sexuality is in the heart. The question is, "What is the condition of my heart?"

CONTROL

The Gospel accounts reveal the teaching of Jesus, which are filled with "heart language." The Pharisees became frustrated after an all-day controversy with Jesus over Sabbath day rules. They accuse Jesus of being sourced by the power of the devil (Matthew 12:24). Jesus answered their accusation by discussing the heart, the source of all actions. He used illustrations like trees bearing fruit (Matthew 12:33). *"For out of the abundance of the heart the mouth speaks. A good man out of the good treasure of his heart brings forth good things, and an evil man out of the evil treasure brings forth evil things"* (Matthew 12:34-35). The mouth speaks from the overflow of the heart. A person does not struggle to know what to speak, looking deep inside and finding nothing, because the heart produces responses, always full and overflowing. The mouth opens and outflows the content of the heart. The heart is in control!

On another occasion, a controversy about defilement rules arose between Jesus and the Pharisees. At the end of the discussion the disciples were afraid that Jesus had offended the Pharisees (Matthew 5:12). *"So Jesus said, 'Are you also still without understanding? Do you not yet understand that whatever enters the mouth goes into the stomach and is eliminated? But those things which proceed out of the mouth come from the heart, and they defile a man. For out of the heart proceed evil thoughts, murders, adulteries, fornications, thefts, false witness, blasphemies'"* (Matthew 15:16-19).

The passages we have just quoted are all repeats of our present passage (Matthew 5:28). The main problem, according to Jesus, is the condition of the heart. *"Those of old"* approached their sexuality as a body appetite to be curbed, requiring discipline. The best they could accomplish was, *"You shall not commit adultery."* The New Covenant is a new way of living. The fullness of the Spirit of Jesus comes to fill the poverty stricken, the helpless heart. When man's helplessness merges with Jesus' nature, the heart takes on a new condition. We become the expression of God's nature. Our sexuality is now filled with the mind of Christ. "Looks" are not the problem! "Lust" is not the problem. What is in control gives expression through the heart. "Lust" is a sourcing issue!

7

ESSENTIALITY:
SEVERITY

MATTHEW 5:29-30

"If your right eye causes you to sin, pluck it out and cast it from you; for it is more profitable for you that one of your members perish than for your whole body to be cast into hell. And if your right hand causes you to sin, cut it off and cast it from you; for it is more profitable for you that one of your members perish, than for your whole body to be cast into hell" (Matthew 5: 29-30).

Jesus' message is focused and deliberate. His opening verse is dedicated to the perspective of *"those of old"* (Matthew 5:27). Thinking they could never achieve the holiness of God and excusing their inability, *"those of old"* misinterpreted the seventh commandment, *"Thou shalt not commit adultery."* Then Jesus gives His perspective, which is a Spirit-filled man, sourced by God's nature (Matthew 5:28). Adultery is not an act of the physical body but the condition of the inner heart. Sexuality filled with self-sourcing pollutes the life, causing lust in what is seen.

Now Jesus moves on in His message (Matthew 5:29-30), intending to shock, disturb, and frighten the listener to a radical consideration of truth. He gives three concepts that underlie two identical statements. One is ESSENTIALITY of Spirit-sourced sexuality, forcefully highlighting the condition of the heart. Your spiritual life is more important than anything else! Second, Jesus proposes the ETERNALNESS of the physical body and the link of the spiritual with the physical going beyond the limits of time, an eternal experience. His third element is the EFFECTS of self-sourced sexuality in life. He leaves us without doubt about the severity of His statements as He boldly gives the consequences of self-sourcing. He has no judgment from His heart but reveals His dread and fear about self-sourcing in our lives!

The idea for our present study is the ESSENTIALITY of Spirit-sourced sexuality. Anything we say in this study will be far inferior to Jesus' intention! There is no way we can exaggerate what Jesus says, which may be the reason He uses such illustrations. His cry is, "Nothing is as essential as your spiritual heart condition." His desire is that we respond to His call to spiritual reality despite the cost. We must sacrifice everything; nothing is more valuable than your spiritual heart!

Let us begin with the *"severity"* of Jesus' presentation. At first these two verses seem out of place (Matthew 5:29-30). Is Jesus contradicting Himself? *"Those of old"* placed sexuality within the boundaries of a physical law regulating physical action. Jesus said the problem of spiritual adultery was a matter of the heart. He placed our sexuality in the core of our being and not in the physical eye or hand. Why does He now speak to us about fleshly things?

The TONE of these two verses is important. Jesus words are intense, and no one listening could miss the seriousness in His voice. He is not speaking casually or making a suggestion. I am certain His listeners felt the pressing penetration of His eye contact, and each person felt like they were the only one in the crowd. The Spirit of God surely took these words and drove them into the heart of each listener.

"If your right eye causes you to sin, pluck it out and cast it from you." Does this need an explanation? The Greek word "exaireo," translated *"pluck it out,"* is in the imperative mood, followed by the Greek word "ballo," translated *"cast it."* Other versions of the Bible translate "exaireo" as "gouge it out" and "ballo" as "throw it out" or "throw it." This language expresses the tone and severity of the problem with sexuality.

"And if your right hand causes you to sin, cut it off and cast it from you." Do we not understand this statement? The Greek word "ekkopson," translated "cut it off," is in the imperative mood, followed by the Greek word "ballo," translated *"cast it."* Jesus' severe tone makes His message loud and clear. Whatever He intends by these statements, He is serious.

The severity of Jesus' intent is not only in His TONE, but also in the fact that His instructions were to *"cast it"* TWICE. Two of the four verses in this illustration go to this severity. You might think that Jesus should have given more explanation to the "looking," "lusting," and "committing" at the heart of the illustration. Matthew wrote this under the inspiration of the Holy Spirit, evidently believing the instructions about the heart condition were adequate. He did not belabor the point but knew his readers needed to understand the severity and importance of the heart's sourcing. The twist of self-centeredness in the heart determines the flow of sexuality in the life. Self-centered sexuality will destroy everything in its path including itself. The Spirit of Jesus must be the source of the life; therefore, sexuality must have the mind of Christ. We cannot overstate this reality!

Jesus states the severity twice in our passage and once later in the Book of Matthew. Jesus teaches His disciples the principles of the cross style (Matthew 16). The last six months of His earthly life and ministry were dedicated to this subject and His twelve disciples. They needed to understand His Messianic role. But the disciples were like the crowds, thinking only of the miracles, power, and position. Jesus is a bleeding, suffering, and dying Messiah. He gives them the first prediction of His death and resurrection (Matthew 16:21).

Moses and Elijah visit with Jesus at the Mount of Transfiguration (Matthew 17:3). Their conversation is a verification of the cross style (Luke 9:31). The law and the prophets (Old Testament Scriptures) testify to this plan. The Father overshadowed the mountain to relay a message to everyone, gave His approval to His Son, and insisted that the disciples listen to Jesus (Matthew 17:5). As Jesus, Peter, James, and John made their way down the mountain, they discussed the coming of the forerunner to the Messiah. The three disciples were unaware that this one called Elijah had already come. They did not recognize John the Baptist as the forerunner of the Messiah. He did no miracles and his ministry ended abruptly with his tragic death! They did not identify John's ministry style with the style of Messiah, but Jesus told them this tragic death was exactly what would happen to Him (Matthew 16:21). John the Baptist verified the cross style by bleeding, suffering, and dying. The nine other disciples left at the base of the mountain failed to deliver a demon-possessed boy. When Jesus arrived He quickly delivered the demon from this young man's life. The disciples asked Jesus privately why they had failed. The answer was obvious; they had failed to embrace the new truth of the cross style (Matthew 17:20). There is no Kingdom ministry outside of the cross style!

Jesus' teaching sessions for the disciples were intended to bring them to the mind of Christ. Instead of heeding His words, the disciples disputed everything He told them. Each disciple was upset and filled with argument regarding their positions in the kingdom of heaven (Matthew 18:1). Each disciple saw himself better than the others, signifying they did not grasp the heart of the Kingdom. What would it take for them to see? Jesus began His instructions again, illustrating the heart of the New Covenant with a child. This child had no rights and could make no demands. He asked for nothing as He snuggled against Jesus' chest in intimate relationship. The surrender of personal rights and losing your life is the standard of the Kingdom (Matthew 18:3).

Then Jesus gives a strong warning to these self-focused disciples. He begins discussing the immature ones just beginning their Christian faith. He warns the disciples about offending one of these (Matthew 18:6). He describes a trap with the trigger set for destruction. Jesus uses the Greek word "skandalise," which is the stick in the trap that causes the destruction and death of its victim. Self-centeredness is like this stick in the trap. Self-centeredness produces handles that the devil can use to control us, causing our actions to destroy the little ones. Like the disciples, we can continue to follow Jesus arguing about our position but little ones will be ruined in the process.

At the moment Jesus gives his self-centered disciples a strong warning, He gives the same two verses in our passage (Matthew 5:29-30). The words are the same except He changes *"right hand"* to *"hand or foot"* and *"right eye"* to *"eye"* (Matthew 18:8-9). In our passage Jesus focuses on "sexuality" (Matthew 5:29-30). Now Jesus focuses on "destroying a little one" (Matthew 18:8-9). What is the connection between these two passages that gave Jesus the right to repeat these two verses of severity?

Maybe you think these are two different subjects. Is the real issue the self-centeredness governing the heart? Self-centeredness dominates the heart that produces sexuality. Sexuality expresses itself in every area of life. My sexuality determines how I walk, my approach to situations, my style of dress, my involvement in relationships, and even seeking positions. The disciples were asking like men, expressing their masculinity, but their sexuality was filled with self-centeredness. What governs the heart dominates sexuality and will cause the person to seek positions. These are not two different subjects at all!

Jesus emphasizes the severity of self-centered sexuality in our passage. He sets the "TONE" of the passage, gives it "TWICE," and the "TIMING" of the passage verifies the statements of these two verses, conveying that the action of the severity should happen immediately. He does not suggest hesitation, and He does not advise six months of counseling, a forty-day fast, or spiritual discipline classes. He is bold and to the point. In other words, self-centeredness governing the heart creates action through our sexuality that cannot be tolerated. This message is urgent!

The obvious urgency is in the "damage" being done by the self-centered expression. The nature of sin, self-centeredness, permeates the heart. It does not abide there in idleness or neutrality. Self-centeredness overtakes the expression of the heart, which Jesus strongly tells us. If the heart is filled with self-focus, the expression of our sexuality will be self-centeredness. This self-centeredness is not limited to the view of *"those of old."* We cannot limit self-centered sexuality to lusting for a woman in a sexual encounter. Self-centered sexuality moves through every area of masculinity and femininity. Self-centeredness shows up in my cocky walk. I demand my preference not only with my wife but also with my children, my business associates, and in all other relationships. Self-centeredness affects the way I dress, style my hair, and present myself. My life thrives on the fulfillment of gratification, as I demand position and self-recognition. Although Jesus highlights specifically the damage done to the opposite sex (Matthew 5:27-30), it is just as true in my relationship with other disciples in decisions and positions (Matthew 18:1). Self-centeredness dominates my heart and sources the sexuality in my life!

The fallout of self-centered domination is inevitable and incredible. Its destruction is progressive, destroying my relationships repeatedly. Jesus quickly moves to a third illustration of higher righteousness exceeding that of the scribes and Pharisees. It is the illustration of marriage

(Matthew 5:31-32). The expression of self-centered sexuality always destroys marriage. Self-centered sexuality never bleeds, suffers, or dies, which is the cross style. The self-centered argument over position and power always brings division in relationships. We do not divide when each of us wants the other to be fulfilled and experience the destiny of God for their life. We divide over what we think we want and need. The same self-centered sexuality destroys our homes, our careers, and our friendships.

Jesus wants all to know the ultimate destruction of self-centeredness. It is *"hell."* Any idea that "hell" will be a fulfillment of our self-centered dreams and a fun party is not in these verses. The severity is in the idea that self-centeredness must be eliminated from our hearts. There is no sacrifice great enough to escape this damage. In each picture, Jesus expresses *"cast it from you."* In other words, whatever self-centeredness uses to bring destruction to your life, you must cut it off and get rid of it. Nothing is worth the present and future destruction of self-centeredness.

The urgency here is that we understand the "designs" of self-centeredness that establishes a permanency in our lives. The severity of self-centered sexuality is in long-range patterns entrenched in the heart of a person. *"Those of old"* had the opposite idea, thinking if they controlled the expression of their body's appetite, "not committing adultery," they could maintain their righteousness. Jesus was concerned with the self-centeredness in the heart, establishing patterns of self-centeredness in the thought process. The self-centered heart dominates the thought process with the desire to use another for personal satisfaction. The cross style pattern is the opposite of self-centeredness. "Lust" cannot thrive on "How can I meet your need?" "Lust" establishes a pattern of abuse as it expresses self-centeredness. "Lust" sees abuse residing in the person who does not meet my needs; they made me do it. Sometimes to even tolerate or receive abuse is self-centeredness. Such a person is not thinking of getting help for their abuser; they are thinking of their need for self and security.

Self-centeredness dominates the heart, and the heart produces sexuality. The designs of self-centeredness become dominate and ingrained in the expressions of the person. Every expression of my masculinity or femininity becomes self-centered. The self-centeredness that produces lust for my neighbor's wife is the same self-centeredness that produced the disciples' desires to dominate their brothers. The argument they had over which of them would be number one was a product of the same design.

Jesus wants us to know that the ultimate deepening and penetration of self-centeredness in our lives will destroy us. He sees the long-range establishment of *"hell."* His view is not one of punishment because we are self-centered but that self-centeredness can overcome our lives. If self-centeredness dominates your sexuality, it expresses itself in every thought and act of your life. Self-centeredness in its final state of growth and fulfillment is *"hell."* When this nature grows through your system and takes over, that is *"hell."* There will never be a better time than now to break the binding control of self-centeredness. It is the plea of Jesus as He calls us to the righteousness of the New Covenant, the indwelling of God's nature.

8

ESSENTIALITY: STUMBLING

MATTHEW 5:29-30

"If your right eye causes you to sin, pluck it out and cast it from you; for it is more profitable for you that one of your members perish than for your whole body to be cast into hell. And if your right hand causes you to sin, cut it off and cast it from you; for it is more profitable for you that one of your members perish, than for your whole body to be cast into hell" (Matthew 5: 29-30).

How do you awaken a person sleeping soundly in a burning house? How do you warn someone about to walk over a precipice? How do you get the attention of a fisherman in a boat headed for the falls? What voice do you use when speaking to an addict destroying himself with drugs or alcohol? How do you stop the person flirting with sin? Is the gentle approach adequate in each of these cases? Is it okay to yell in desperation? In our passage Jesus' method is the use of extreme illustrations. He uses violent speech!

Jesus uses instructive verbs, all imperative, in each of His statements, giving the instruction a sense of command, order, and urgency. The logic of His statements has an explanation of urgency. The foundation of His logic is eternal life, taking on a tone of loving compassion. He is not judgmental or condemning in His approach, but He pleads with us to follow His instruction so we will not end in hell, highlighting the emotional involvement coming from His heart of love.

He gives three elements underlying these two identical statements. The first is ESSENTIALITY of Spirit-sourced sexuality, giving the condition of the heart importance. The value of your spiritual life is greater than anything else! He brings into focus the ETERNALNESS of our physical bodies. He links the spiritual intimately with the physical, going beyond the limits of time in an eternal experience. In His third consideration, He warns that the EFFECTS of self-sourced sexuality are a danger to our lives. He so boldly tells of the consequences of self-sourcing that we can feel the severity of His instructions. He has no judgment or condemnation coming from His heart, but we can sense His dread and fear that such will happen in our lives!

The concept for our present study is the ESSENTIALITY of Spirit-sourced sexuality. We will not be able to match the level of these statements. Nothing we can say will equal the forceful yet simple, concise statements of Jesus. My fear is that what we say about them will only degrade the intensity and emphasis Jesus intended. He cries out to us, "Nothing is as essential as the spiritual condition of your heart." He calls us to spiritual success regardless of the cost. Nothing has more value, which means we can sacrifice everything for the sake of our spiritual victory.

Our concentration in our previous study was on the **severity** of these statements, found in the "tone" of Jesus' words. The grammar and general focus of His statements present urgency. The statements are given "twice," which highlights the severity. Jesus presents these statements twice in our passage, but these statements appear one other time in Matthew's Gospel (Matthew 18:8-9). The "timing" of the statements presses us to the urgency of what we must do immediately. There is no room for neglect.

Now we come to the second aspect of the ESSENTIALITY of Spirit-sourced sexuality; it is the *"stumbling block."* You must not be naïve! Never let yourself think there is no enemy. The evil one fights to destroy you because he knows how valuable and important the Spirit-sourced life is! The two statements in our passage are tied to *"looks"* (Matthew 5:28). The Spirit of Jesus determines the view of what we see. We do not always have control over what we see, but the condition of our hearts determines how we think about what we see. The spiritual battle rages on the level of our viewpoint. Will we embrace the mind of Christ?

Jesus speaks with a definite "TONE" in regard to the enemy and the possibility of **stumbling**. He uses the Greek word "skandalizo," translated *"causes you to sin."* In the Greek text, the word **"sin"** is not present; but was placed there in the English to give the idea of the Greek word. This verb is in the active voice and must be treated in the causative sense. It means, "to offend, lead astray, or lead into sin." The act of offending is not to upset, annoy, vex, or irritate; rather, the context of the word is one of violence, destruction, or ruin.

We must not think the English word *"causes"* should be interpreted as "makes" or "forces" someone to sin. "Skandalizo" is the picture of the trigger in a death trap not the wire that forms the cage of the trap, or the bait that lures the animal into the trap, but the stick that holds the door in place. Once the animal enters the cage and disturbs the stick, the door swings shut and kills the animal. In a mousetrap this word refers not to the wood forming the base, or the cheese attracting the mouse, but is the strong wire that holds the spring in place. Once that spring is disturbed, the trap is sprung and the mouse dies.

In our passage Jesus refers to the *"right eye"* and the *"right hand"* as the stick in the death trap. Your eye or your hand cannot destroy your life. These body parts are not sinful and should not be discarded. In this illustration the eye and the hand are symbolic of anything that is used to trap you in a sinful state. Jesus ties these body parts to the sexuality, because "looking" is a function of the eye, Jesus begins with the *"right eye."* The eye is not sinful, because there is nothing sinful about looking, but adultery occurs in the motive of the looking. If the motive of the looking is a product of the heart, should we cut out our heart and cast it from us? No, because the physical heart is not sinful. It is the sinful nature that controls the core of a person.

When we are mastered by our self-centeredness, it infiltrates and dominates our sexuality, which expresses itself in our lives. How can you *"pluck it out and cast it from you?"* We have to take another look at the premise of the Sermon on the Mount. We are helpless, without resource (Matthew 5:3). Will we embrace this helplessness as a mother embraces her grief over losing her child

(Matthew 5:4)? When we surrender, we will spiritually experience the equivalent to *"cut it off and cast it from you."* Jesus can then deliver us from ourselves and fill us with His nature! We have to lose ourselves to save ourselves, not just the eye or the hand. It is a desperate measure.

How can I be sure this surrender is true? Jesus repeated it "TWICE," once for the right eye and again for the right hand. Matthew also records Jesus making these references later in another crucial scene (Matthew 18:9-10). In the context of these two statements and after six months of Jesus' ministry with the disciples, He works to prepare them for the coming crucifixion, predicting His death and resurrection three times (Matthew 16:21; 17:22; 20:18). He describes to them the Kingdom of God, but they argue with Him about this for six days. Their self-centeredness keeps them from accepting the bleeding, suffering, and dying of the cross. Even after Moses and Elijah confirm this truth at the Mount of Transfiguration (Matthew 17:3), God, the Father, assures them of this truth (Matthew 17:5). John the Baptist foreran this reality (Matthew 17:11), and the disciples experienced failure in ministry because of their arguing (Matthew 17:20), they still do not understand.

The disciples reveal their self-centeredness when they come to Jesus, arguing among themselves and demanding He choose one of them for the number one position in the Kingdom (Matthew 18:1). Jesus tells them that they must become like the child sitting on His lap (Matthew 18:2-5). This child is a symbol of helplessness, especially in the culture of Jesus where children had no status. The child is in love with Jesus, and he makes no attempt to do anything on his own. Can we do the same?

Jesus begins to warn the disciples of the consequences of continuing in their self-centeredness. He said, ***"Whoever causes one of these little ones who believe in Me to sin, it would be better for him if a millstone were hung around his neck, and he were drowned in the depth of the sea"*** (Matthew 18:6). He uses the Greek word "skandalizo," translated ***"causes...to sin."*** Self-centeredness gives Satan a foothold in our lives, which he can then use as "a stick in a death trap" for someone who embraces Jesus in helplessness.

Jesus goes on to make an even stronger statement, saying, ***"Woe to the world because of offenses! For offenses must come, but woe to that man by whom the offense comes!"*** (Matthew 18:7). The Greek word "skandalizo," translated ***"offenses,"*** is the same word He uses in the previous verse. Jesus warns of many "sticks in death traps" in our world, but we must never be one of them. We cannot tolerate self-centeredness in our lives. Then Jesus repeats to the disciples the two verses from our passage (Matthew 18:8-9).

The same self-centeredness that controls our sexuality expresses itself by demanding position and lording itself over others. Self-centered sexuality will always express itself through self-centered masculinity. The disciples demanded power and control over others. This self-centeredness is a "stick in a death trap," and it will always cause us to sin. In other words, our self-centeredness becomes a trap for others as well as for ourselves. We must allow Jesus to eliminate it; we can never tolerate or control it. We must surrender to Jesus as our only source and embrace our helplessness, whatever the cost.

Jesus gives us a prime example of this in the first

prediction of His death and resurrection (Matthew 16:21). He opens His heart to His disciples with the expectation that they will have open and teachable spirits. ***"Then Peter took Him aside and began to rebuke Him, saying, 'Far be it from You, Lord; this shall not happen to You!'"*** (Matthew 16:22). Peter did not say that He did not believe Jesus was the Messiah, but he rebuked Jesus because he did not see Jesus as the kind of Messiah He was describing. In Peter's mind the Messiah who would deliver Israel could never bleed, suffer, or die. That was not the style of the Messiah. ***"But He turned and said to Peter, 'Get behind Me, Satan! You are an offense to Me, for you are not mindful of the things of God, but the things of men'"*** (Matthew 16:23). Satan was using Peter to set a trap for Jesus, and Peter had become a "stick in a death trap" for Jesus. Peter became an instrument of the devil.

Returning to our passage, how could Jesus have been more serious with His warning? What other words could He have used to impact us? Self-centeredness controls the heart and will use sexuality to set "a stick in a death trap" for those around us, trapping them and us. Would it be easier to pluck out our right eye or cut off our right hand than to surrender our lives? We must embrace our helplessness as if overcome with grief. There are no traps in surrender. When we are filled with God's nature we know only His freedom and victory!

"TIMING" is another element to consider in **stumbling**. The Greek word "skandalizo," translated ***"causes... to sin,"*** is in the present tense. In the Greek language, the present tense is used when the writer portrays an action in process or a state of being with no assessment of the action's completion. In other words, the action of the verb happens at the present moment and continues into the future, an ongoing experience. The action of the verb happens in this present moment, but when this moment becomes a past moment, the action moves into the new present moment. The reality of being "a stick in a death trap" is not something that happened and is now behind us; it is not contained in the boundaries of one evening, a single event, or a moment of weakness. "A stick in a death trap" is an ongoing, always present, occurrence in life.

Our self-centeredness grips and controls the heart flow into our sexuality. Self-centered sexuality continually moves in the activity of being "a stick in a death trap." Self-centeredness is always baiting, alluring, and trapping. This self-centered sexuality is easy to understand in the life of a prostitute because dress, mannerisms, speech, walking and tone of life are to allure and trap. The self-centered prostitute uses sexuality as "a stick in a death trap." We are quick to say, "I am not that way!" Although this may be true in our intent, is it true of our nature? Could it be true that self-centeredness expresses itself throughout your sexuality by dominating your spouse, demanding your own way, becoming angry with your boss, or a thousand other expressions? Perhaps it is not a single expression that you can eliminate, but a tone of your life that is present tense with continual action throughout your life.

If there is any possibility of this being true, can I eliminate it? If every expression of my life is under the control of self-centered sexuality, am I capable of recognizing my condition? How can I take my thousands of self-centered expressions and surrender my heart condition? I can only adjust, compromise, and excuse my actions. My only victory comes in embracing my helplessness and allowing Jesus to conquer my heart!

Self-centered sexuality seems to be a key issue! We often substitute religious reform for crucifixion. We tackle the obvious expressions of self-centered sexuality and admire ourselves for our achievement. We become examples of discipline and religious success. However, these may only be another form of the same self-centered sexuality of the prostitute. These forms being the same is why Jesus was so radical in His imperatives insisting that all expressions of self-centered sexuality have to come to an end. When we approach sexuality as a body drive that can be expressed only within the boundary of not committing adultery, our self-centered sexuality will dominate our lives in all our expressions, and we never confront our heart problem.

Jesus calls us to righteousness beyond the righteousness of the scribes and Pharisees (Matthew 5:20). Religious reform is not His challenge. His premise is that we must embrace our helplessness, and to do this we must abandon the self-centeredness determined to seek only for self. The problem is that we are not capable of this. We are so dominated by self-centeredness that we cannot adequately surrender. Will you join me in posturing ourselves in humility and admit our helplessness? Will we allow the Spirit of Jesus to crucify our self-centeredness and fill us with His nature? This is our only salvation!

9

ESSENTIALITY: SPIRITUAL PRIORITY

MATTHEW 5:29-30

"If your right eye causes you to sin, pluck it out and cast it from you; for it is more profitable for you that one of your members perish than for your whole body to be cast into hell. And if your right hand causes you to sin, cut it off and cast it from you; for it is more profitable for you that one of your members perish, than for your whole body to be cast into hell" (Matthew 5: 29-30).

Some things are a mystery, "something that cannot be understood unless someone reveals it to you." Paul used the word often to describe things in the spiritual realm of life (Romans 11:25; 16:25; 1 Corinthians 2:7; 15:51; Ephesians 1:9; 3:3; 5:32; 6:19; Colossians 1:26-27). Jesus used the word "mystery" regarding the Kingdom of Heaven, using parables to reveal *"the mysteries of the kingdom of heaven"* (Matthew 13:11). In the New Testament, the idea of "mysteries" relates to aspects of the spiritual. Although we may not know everything, we can know something!

Our physical sexuality definitely exposes a spiritual mystery. Although other areas of our physical may not reveal the spiritual, that is not true of our sexuality. In this section of the Sermon on the Mount, Jesus gives six illustrations (Matthew 5:21-48), but the illustration of sexuality is the only one where He highlights the heart. The sexuality in my life is distinctly connected to the spiritual.

"Those of old" isolated their sexuality to a simple body appetite they maintained with a law, *"You shall not commit adultery"* (Matthew 5:27). But the New Covenant Man, filled with the Spirit, sees sexuality from a spiritual perspective (Matthew 5:28). That which controls the "heart" controls the "looking." If the heart is self-centered, then every aspect of sexuality is self-centered; the way we walk, talk, flirt, think, see, and act. Adultery happens in the spiritual realm of the heart long before it expresses itself in the physical. We must be filled with the Spirit of Jesus to refrain from adultery.

How serious is this issue? Jesus is serious when He launches into the two verses of our passage (Matthew 5:29-30). The tone of His words is equivalent to "yelling," "pressing," or "demanding," and is filled with urgency, indicating priority. There are three major ideas underlying these two statements. One is the ESSENTIALITY of Spirit-sourced sexuality. Jesus was forceful about the importance of the inner heart's condition. Your spiritual life is above all else in importance! Secondly,

He proposed bringing into focus the ETERNALNESS of the physical body. The intimate link of the spiritual with the physical goes far beyond the limits of time; it is eternal. His third consideration regards the EFFECTS of self-sourced sexuality in life. He boldly says the consequences of self-sourcing are severe. There is no judgment or condemnation from His heart. He fears these effects will happen in our lives!

The idea for our present study is the ESSENTIALITY of Spirit-sourced sexuality. We must set aside everything to experience victory in our sexuality. In a previous study, we concentrated on the **severity** of Jesus' statements, His "tone." The grammar and focus of the statements present His urgency. He gives each statement "twice," which highlights the severity. He repeats these statements in a later encounter with His disciples (Matthew 18:8-9). The "timing" of the statements presses us to the urgency of what we must do immediately. There is no room for neglect.

We also considered the **stumbling block**. Do not be naïve! Never forget there is an enemy! He is fighting to destroy you! Only the Spirit-sourced life can keep you in victory. The "tone" of the blockage is in the Greek word "skandalizo," translated *"causes... sin."* "Skandalizo" is the stick in a death trap. Jesus emphasizes this "twice" in our passage and "twice" again in a dispute among the disciples (Matthew 18:8-9). The "timing" of the verb is present tense with continual action. This offense is not an event but a continual alluring or entrapment. The **severity** is connected to the **stumbling block**. The only safe place is in Jesus!

The third aspect of ESSENTIALITY of the Spirit-sourced

sexuality is **spiritual priority**. This aspect introduces us to the "mystery" of the Kingdom of God. In the Scriptures an explanation of a spiritual mystery is most often given in the physical. We see this in the parables of Jesus. He explained the Kingdom of God and its spiritual involvement through farming (Matthew 13). The mystery of Jesus' relationship with His bride, the Church, is seen through the physical relationship of marriage (Ephesians 5:32). In our passage, Jesus declared the value of our spiritual lives by comparing it to valuable body parts.

Jesus highlighted the priority of our spiritual lives through the "tone" of the passage. The suggestion of plucking out the right eye or cutting off the right hand suggests a violent act of desperation. The Greek word "exaireo," translated *"pluck out,"* is a compound word, "ek" meaning "from," a movement term, and "haireo" meaning "to take." You would think the suggestion of the violent act of gouging out your eye would be enough to establish the priority of the spiritual parallel. But Jesus added the phrase, *"and cast it from you"* (Matthew 5:29). This adds another dimension to the violent desperation of the act. Jesus demanded that the instrument of the body that becomes "a stick in a death trap" should not only be gouged out but also thrown far from you. You are to despise this as despicable, contemptible, and loathsome. You are not to treasure it, save it, or have longings for it.

Gouging out your eye should be enough to convince you of His intent, but Jesus continued with another example of the right hand. If your right hand becomes "a stick in a death trap," you must *"cut it off,"* another violent picture. This command is the compound Greek word "ekkopto," which combines "ek" meaning "from or out," a movement term, and "kopto" meaning "to cut." The picture Jesus offers again is unthinkable, the violent act of chopping off your hand. This should convince us that the spiritual realm is far superior in importance to the physical realm. But as before, Jesus adds the statement, *"and cast it from you"* (Matthew 5:30). You must not compromise or hesitate. Any thought of saving or cherishing the hand after cutting it off must be renounced. You are to view it as an instrument of evil to be eliminated.

The Greek word "ballo," translated *"cast,"* is specific. It is used twenty-five times in the New Testament and most often has the tone of violence. However, there is a definite tone each time it is used, the tone of "impulsiveness." We see this in the temptations of Jesus that occurred immediately after He was filled with the Holy Spirit. The devil conveyed Him to the pinnacle of the temple in the holy city (Matthew 4:5). Jesus was ready to launch His earthly ministry and fulfill the call of the Father. What would be His first official act of ministry? The devil suggested a method of sure success, *"If you are the Son of God, throw Yourself down"* (Matthew 4:6). The devil based this suggestion on two Scriptures. The Greek word "ballo," translated *"thrown down,"* carries the suggestion of "impulsiveness." Do not hesitate, do not think about it, and do not consult the Father. Just "do it."

This impulsiveness is the indication in our passage as well! In regard to our spiritual lives, we must not hesitate. We must do whatever is necessary to secure and maintain spiritual victory! We do not need to counsel, discuss, or contemplate the need. The value of your spiritual life is so far superior to the physical realm that it presents no contest. Everything must be treated as insignificant compared to the spiritual. Jesus is the only One to have our focus. Do not allow anything to hinder your seeking Him. He is not a means to an end; He is *the* means and *the* end. He must capture you and me!

Listen to Paul's heart: *"But what things were gain to me, these I have counted loss for Christ. Yet indeed I also count all things loss for the excellence of the knowledge of Christ Jesus my Lord, for whom I have suffered the loss of all things, and count them as rubbish, that I may gain Christ and be found in Him"* (Philippians 3:7-9). The Greek word "skubalon," translated *"rubbish,"* is a compound word, "kusi" that is plural for dogs and "ballo" meaning "to cast." "Skubalon" is the refuse cast off to the packs of wild dogs that feed on the garbage of the city. This is the call of our verse. Everything must be considered unimportant in comparison to your spiritual life. No pride, no relationship, no material thing, no emotional feeling, no tradition, or any other thing will keep me from Him!

We must understand these statements in light of this reality. *"Who shall separate us from the love of Christ? Shall tribulation, or distress, or persecution, or famine, or nakedness, or peril, or sword? As it is written: 'For Your sake we are killed all day long; we are accounted as sheep for the slaughter.' Yet is all these things we are more than conquerors through Him who loved us. For I am persuaded that neither death nor life, nor angels nor principalities nor powers, nor things present nor thing to come, nor height nor depth, nor any other created thing, shall be able to separate us from the love of God which is in Christ Jesus our Lord"* (Romans 8:35-39). Jesus is our priority. We will pluck out, cut off, and cast from us everything to be His!

Jesus used **spiritual priority** "twice" in our passage sharing the two examples of the *"right eye"* and *"right hand."* The significance is not in the body part; it is in the emphasis on *"right,"* signifying the "instrument of performance!" For instance, in important transactions when action must be determined, resolute, and involve the full participation of the doer, the right hand is used. Also when the full energy and emphasis of a person are intended, the right hand is used (Revelation 1:16, 17, 20; 2:1; 5:1, 7). The right eye or right hand becomes the symbol of focus for the total person.

In this illustration, Jesus' message is that my sexuality has spiritual priority. Sexuality is not one among many body drives I can control with a rule. Sexuality is integrated into every aspect of my life, rooted in the heart, the core of my being. Sexuality flows into every expression of my being and has high priority because it controls the action of my life in the spiritual realm, expressing itself in the physical realm. Jesus spoke about the right eye and right hand, confronting the expression of my being. Sexuality has spiritual priority. Whatever it takes for my life to be filled with the Spirit of Jesus, I must do it. Jesus not only expressed this in words but also physically gave Himself. I must do the same!

Jesus' emphasis on *"right"* also signifies the "instrument of power!" The whole person is claimed by the right hand, whether in action or in suffering (Psalms 109:6, 31; Acts 2:25). The significance is not on the body part but on the person's power of expression. Sexuality is the power basis of our manipulation of each other and the basis of advertisement and selling. Sexuality is an instrument of manipulation in marriage. We use sexuality as a bargaining tool to dominate and secure our own way. No wonder Jesus cried out about this flow of power in our lives. The problem is not in the power of our sexuality because our sexuality is a result of our creation. The problem is in what nature controls this power. Are we filled with self-centeredness or the Spirit of Jesus? This filling is the heart of our spiritual priority.

The biblical "instrument of position" is the *"right."* A person of high rank who puts someone on his right hand gives him equal honor with himself and recognizes him with equal dignity (Matthew 20:21, 23; 22:44; 26:64; 27:38). Jesus sees our sexuality as an expression of this honor. In marriage extreme honor is placed on the woman. As the husband honors his own flesh, so he honors his wife. Paul uses the imagery of Jesus' relationship and involvement with the church. The husband is to love his wife as his own body; he loves his wife as he loves himself (Ephesians 5:28-31). Jesus again highlights spiritual priority. Our spiritual nature, which controls our sexuality, determines the honor and value of our sexuality.

Jesus climaxed each of these statements with the issue of "timing." Spiritual priority is determined by "timing." Sexuality dominated by self-centeredness is temporary; it will destroy itself. Self-sourced sexuality soon finds the years have passed, and the beauty and sexual attractiveness a person dedicated themselves to have slipped away. The spiritual life that matters forever was neglected. It does not take long until we say, "I used to." I used to be a star; I used to hold the high position; I used to impress people with my looks. Life quickly becomes a memory of what we used to do and be, and it is an expression of sexuality filled with self.

Although the illustration Jesus uses is physical (eye or hand), the issue is the spiritual. We must apply the logic of the physical world to the spiritual world. It is better to be without an eye or hand in this physical life than for your whole body to perish in spiritual hell. The priority is not in the physical but in the spiritual. These two verses bring into perspective the contrast between *"those of old"* (Matthew 5:27) and *"But I say to you"* (Matthew 5:28). This contrast is not a discussion about controlling a body appetite with a rule. Sexuality is an issue of the heart that flows from the core of mankind into every expression of life. Our thinking, perspective, approach, walk, talk, dress, attitude, how we respond, what we eat, and what we desire are all influenced by our sexuality. This influence comes from the helpless heart, and this heart will be controlled either by the nature of Jesus or by our self-centeredness. This control is a spiritual issue.

These two verses cry out the *severity* of our situation. We cannot control our sexuality by a rule about physical activity. We must approach our sexuality with a spirit of desperation. Sexuality is not one problem among many, but it is many problems brought down to the single problem of our nature. We must overcome or eliminate every **stumbling block**. The Spirit of Jesus will enable us. Nothing can stop us from being His. A new nature is ours for the asking; we can be reborn! Do not be fooled by the emphasis of old on a rule about a physical appetite. This new nature is a **spiritual priority.** This is not about a moment or moments of pleasure, but it is the fulfillment of our lives forever. Jesus is our new nature!

10

PROPOSITION OF ETERNITY

MATTHEW 5:29-30

"If your right eye causes you to sin, pluck it out and cast it from you; for it is more profitable for you that one of your members perish than for your whole body to be cast into hell. And if your right hand causes you to sin, cut it off and cast it from you; for it is more profitable for you that one of your members perish, than for your whole body to be cast into hell" (Matthew 5: 29-30).

Eternal life is a marvel! Eternity is "the merciful Trinity God giving us a state of blessedness in His presence that endures without end." This state of blessedness is the quality of life in this age and the quality and duration of life in the age to come. Paul highlighted this when he said, *"Blessed be the God and Father of our Lord Jesus Christ, who has blessed us with every spiritual blessing in the heavenly places in Christ"* (Ephesians 1:3).

Bible scholars contradict each other concerning

eternal life in the Old Testament. Some propose the absence of awareness of the eternal state. However, the Old Testament clearly declares, "God is eternal" (Deuteronomy 33:27; Psalms 10:16; 48:14). Our Lord is the Rock Eternal (Isaiah 26:4) and the eternal King (Jeremiah 10:10). God's word, rooted in His being and will, is likewise eternal (Psalms 119:89), as are His righteous laws (Psalms 119:60), His ways (Habakkuk 3:6), and His kingdom or dominion (Daniel 4:3, 34). God is eternal; therefore, His love (1 Kings 10:9), His blessings (Psalms 21:6), and all His attributes and blessings are eternal. As long as God exists, so do they! "His mercy endures forever" is repeated twenty-six times in Psalms (136). "Forever" describes His reign (Psalms 9:7), His protection, (Psalms 12:7), His plan (Psalms 33:11), the inheritance of His people (Psalms 37:18), His throne (Psalms 45:19), His rule (Psalms 66:7), His covenant (Psalms 105:8), His righteousness (Psalms 111:3), His faithfulness (Psalms 117:2), His statutes (Psalms 119:111, 152), and His name (Psalms 135:13).

If God is eternal, what are His children's possibilities? The progressive revelation of the Scriptures brings us into the New Testament view of eternity where eternal life is the dominant theme. Eternity describes the time that God's favor extends to His people, and the quality of existence they are to experience in His fullness. We must not confuse eternal life with endless existence, which all have, saved and unsaved. Natural life is subject to death, and we derive it through human existence. Eternal life comes through the indwelling nature of God's Spirit. Therefore, separation from God is eternal death, and union with Jesus' Spirit is eternal life. Augustine said,

"Join thyself to the eternal God, and thou wilt be eternal."

Nicodemus came to Jesus in the night hour for a conversation on eternal life. The heart of their discussion produced the most memorized verse in the Scriptures. *"And as Moses lifted up the serpent in the wilderness, even so must the Son of Man be lifted up, that whoever believes in Him should not perish but have eternal life. For God so loved the world that He gave His only begotten Son, that whoever believes in Him should not perish but have everlasting life"* (John 3:14-16).

On a journey through Samaria, Jesus talked with a Samaritan woman. He assured her that trust in Him would relieve the thirst of her soul; she would receive, *"a fountain of water springing up into everlasting life"* (John 4:14). Jesus defined eternal life in His high priestly prayer. *"And this is eternal life, that they may know You, the only true God, and Jesus Christ whom You have sent"* (John 17:3). Eternal life results from an intimate relationship with the eternal God!

The Greek word "monai," translated "eternal" or "everlasting," appears six times in the Gospel of Matthew. It is the heart's cry of a Rich Young Ruler who came running to Jesus with a question about his life. *"Good Teacher, what good thing shall I do that I may have eternal life?"* (Matthew 19:16). This encounter between Jesus and the Rich Young Ruler concerned the disciples. They wondered what they should consider since they had left everything to follow Jesus. Jesus said, *"And everyone who has left houses or brothers or sisters or father or mother or wife or children or lands, for My name's sake, shall receive a hundredfold, and inherit eternal life"* (Matthew 19:29).

Jesus emphasized the word eternal in the parable of the

judgment, saying the sheep will be separated from the goats. *"Then He will also say to those on the left hand, 'Depart from Me, you cursed, into the everlasting fire prepared for the devil and his angels"* (Matthew 25:41). The goats will depart because they did not recognize Jesus in the hungry and thirsty around them. The Jesus said, *"And these will go away into everlasting punishment, but the righteous into eternal life"* (Matthew 25:46). In this parable Jesus distinguished the forever life of the unsaved with the eternal life of the saved.

The words "eternal" or "everlasting" are not used in our passage (Matthew 5:29-30). When Jesus quotes this passage a second time, He inserts this word. The disciples were arguing over position, demanding that Jesus choose one of them to be the leader. He urged them to become as little children without rights. If they did not die to their self-centered nature, they would be an offense to the little ones. The results of this were severe and unthinkable. He cried, *"If your hand or foot causes you to sin, cut it off and cast it from you. It is better for you to enter into life lame or maimed, rather than having two hands or two feet, to be cast into the everlasting fire"* (Matthew 18:8). Here Jesus interprets the word *"hell,"* referring to the eternal state of a person.

There is a TONE to our proposition of eternity. In our passage Jesus definitely relies on the logic of the reality of eternity. If you and I are not going to live forever, then Jesus' statement has no impact on us. The logic is that we would be better to spend a few years in this present life without an eye or a hand, than to live eternally in a place of torment with all our body parts intact. However, this makes sense only if we are going to live forever.

Jesus surrounds our sexuality with eternity! His approach revolves around the idea of *"it is more profitable,"* a translation of the Greek word "sumpherei." This word is used in various ways fifteen times in the New Testament. "Sumpherei" is a compound word, "sun" means "to gather," and "phero" means "to bring." However, it is used in this sense only one place in the New Testament (Acts 19:19). The other uses highlight the ideas of "profitable, advantageous, to contribute, to bring together for the benefit of another."

The strength of the Greek word "sumpherei" is found in the context of the passage. Jesus uses this word in exaggerated or outlandish figures of speech. *"Whoever causes one of these little ones who believe in Me to sin, it would be better for him if a millstone were hung around his neck, and he were drowned in the depth of the sea"* (Matthew 18:6). Jesus is not declaring the punishment for offending a little one, rather He suggests that before we offend a little one, we should get a millstone around our neck and drown ourselves. This severe suggestion would be an advantage to us! It is exaggerated language illustrating how profitable it is not to offend a little one.

Jesus gives the disciples and the crowds the binding qualities of oneness in marriage. I must lose my life to enter marriage. The only reason Moses commanded to give a certificate of divorce was because, *"of the hardness of your hearts"* (Matthew 19:8). The disciples' response was revealing. *"If such is the case of the man with his wife, it is better* (sumphero) *not to marry"* (Matthew 19:10). They were saying that there was no profit for them in marriage if they could not use their wives to their advantage. Jesus then uses exaggerated language about the eunuchs (Matthew 19:11-12). Jesus took an unequivocal stance on divorce (no more divorce); this is contrasted with the human excuses (then better for no marriage at all). The difference is that in the first instance there is a genuine "spiritual" advantage or benefit, whereas in the second there is merely an "earthly-human" one.

Jesus uses the same exaggerated and outlandish language in our passage. The suggestion of plucking out your eye and casting it away or cutting off your hand and throwing it is unthinkable. But it is reasonable in light of eternity. If you adequately understand the present in contrast with forever, you would not hesitate. You and I must not be shortsighted by the present. We must see everything in view of eternity!

The advantage is in eternity. Jesus clearly says this in His purpose clause. He introduces eternity with the Greek word "iva," translated "that." The severity of removing everything that blocks my embrace of His resource is for one purpose, for my profit and advantage. The purpose is, **"that one of your members perish, than for your whole body to be cast into hell"** (Matthew 5:29, 30). This issue is eternity! You are going to live forever; what will be the quality of your life? The state of your eternalness is worth every sacrifice in the present. Nothing must hold a higher priority in your life now than your spiritual destiny then!

In greeting another person, we often ask, "How are your doing?" "One day at a time," is a common answer. We are living in the "now" generation because we want everything "now." We determine our priorities by what is pleasurable in the present, what seems acceptable and good for the moment. But this has been a problem for every generation. Jesus struck a blow at the heart of this concept when He declared there is an eternity!

We must understand the proposition of eternity in view of TWICE. In previous studies we discovered that Jesus proposed this idea twice (Matthew 5:29-30). In the first statement the focus regarded *"your right eye"* (Matthew 5:29). In the second statement the focus regarded *"your right hand."* It seems Jesus carefully selected each of these statements concerning sexuality.

There is significance to the *"right eye"* and the *"right hand."* Each *"right"* presents a powerful and important instrument of life, the frontline, and the first body part engaging our sexuality. The *"right eye"* is the power eye and is the eye used for long distance and gives the body a complete view of life. Therefore, the eye conveys the viewpoint affecting the response of the rest of the body, and Jesus suggested it in relation to our sexuality. It is about *"looks," "lust,"* and *"committed."* The eye, under the domination of the heart, controls all this. What if the eye supplies wrong information to the body? Instead of the eye grasping the long-range view for the body, it is shortsighted, seeing only the immediate and inappropriate response.

Jesus pleads with us to have the long-range view. We must see and understand the immediate in light of the eternal. If we sacrifice the eternal future for immediate satisfaction, we are of all people the most miserable. This emphasis was not a single focus for Jesus, but He continually highlighted it in His ministry. Jesus told a parable of a rich man whose crops were in abundance, and he did not have enough room to store them all. His right eye was shortsighted causing him to conclude only one solution; he must pull down his barns and build bigger ones. His larger, well-stocked barns gave him a false sense of security. Thinking he had many goods laid up for years to come, he lounged in his false security. He decided to take his ease, *"eat, drink, and be merry"* (Luke 12:16-21). That night his soul was required of him. What then happened to all the treasure he had stored? His right eye had failed him!

The *"right hand"* is considered to be the hand of power. The "right hand" is used nine times in the Gospel of Matthew; seven of those refer to its power. The mother of two of Jesus' disciples sought the right-hand position for one of her sons (Matthew 20:21). Jesus quoted the Psalms to the Pharisees, *"The Lord said to my Lord, 'sit at My right hand, till I make Your enemies Your footstool'"?* (Matthew 22:44). In the parables of judgment, Jesus spoke of separating the sheep from the goats by placing them on the right hand (Matthew 25:33-34). In the final trials of His life, Jesus said to the Sanhedrin, *"Nevertheless, I say to you, hereafter you will see the Son of Man sitting at the right hand of the Power, and coming on the clouds of heaven"* (Matthew 26:64). The soldiers in the Praetorium mocked Jesus as a King. They put a scarlet robe around His shoulders, a crown of thorns on His head, and a reed in His right hand (Matthew 27:27-31).

The right hand and the right eye are to protect us from the swift approach of eternal hell. But when the right eye fails to see the long-range view and cares only for the moment, you are led astray. When the power of our life (right hand) focuses its strength on the moment and misses the eternal values, you are damned. We are stripped of all caution and cascade through the days of our lives unaware of eternal values. Stop this process; whatever you have to do to gain proper perspective, do it!

We must see the proposition of eternity in light of TIMING. Your sexuality and its expression must never be considered private or without consequence. Is there any doubt that Jesus warns us about present moments affecting eternal moments? As the condition of the heart determines the expressions of our sexuality, so the combined expression of our lives determines the destiny of our eternity. It is as if this present life is a period of probation, which has long-range eternal consequences. This life with all of its involvements sets the stage for the eternity of your life!

These forceful thoughts should produce concern and fear in the hearts of men. The Rich Young Ruler runs to Jesus crying, **"Good Teacher, what good thing shall I do that I may have eternal life?"** (Matthew 19:16). This young man had everything life could offer. He was wealthy and lacked nothing in the materialistic realm. He had position and authority; therefore, he experienced self-esteem and self-worth. Yet, there was a deep-seated awareness that something was missing; there was more involved than just this life. This life with all its involvements is preparatory for the "forever" to come.

"Those of old" viewed their sexuality as an appetite to be regulated and controlled. They placed a boundary around its expression, **"You shall not commit adultery."** Jesus did not give another rule not even an intensified rule, "You shall not look *at a woman to lust for her."* He applied the basic premise of the Sermon on the Mount to the sexuality affecting life. We are **"poor in spirit"**

(Matthew 5:3). We must embrace our helplessness with mourning (Matthew 5:4). When we live in our helplessness, we open the doors of our heart for the Spirit of Jesus to invade our lives, and we become the new creature called *"the kingdom of heaven."* Our helplessness filled with His presence produces a new view of sexuality. We change our dress, our manner of walking, our approach to life, our attitudes, our view of marriage, and the way we treat those of a different gender. Entering this Kingdom of Heaven is the essence of eternal life. We have entered into the spiritual realm of the eternities.

11

PLACES OF ETERNITY

MATTHEW 5:29-30

"If your right eye causes you to sin, pluck it out and cast it from you; for it is more profitable for you that one of your members perish than for your whole body to be cast into hell. And if your right hand causes you to sin, cut it off and cast it from you; for it is more profitable for you that one of your members perish, than for your whole body to be cast into hell" (Matthew 5: 29-30).

To understand any part of the Sermon on the Mount, we must yield to the basic premise of the sermon. Jesus did not give a series of random thoughts. He began with a premise, and every thought that followed complemented the premise. He proposed the helplessness of humanity (Matthew 5:3). We are poor with no resource. He never speaks of our talents, finances, or thoughts; we are poverty stricken in our "spirit." This helplessness is not a result of our sin, but it is the purpose of God's plan for us. We are to embrace this as we embrace the grief of losing a loved one (Matthew 5:4). In this embrace Jesus merges in oneness with us, and together we become the Kingdom of Heaven.

The opposite of this embrace becomes a place called *"hell."* Jesus is implicit about our lack of embrace, and the severity of the passage is contained in this problem. Our sexuality must embrace Jesus in oneness, sacrificing anything that hinders this oneness. Refusing this embrace will bring us to *"hell."* Jesus does not use *"hell"* as a fear technique, but that does not mean it should not frighten us.

It will help us to understand some fundamental biblical definitions. The word "eternity" is a basic idea in the Scriptures, but we may not understand it properly. This English word does not appear anywhere in the New International Version. In the New King James Version (Acts 15:8), it is used once and twice in the New American Standard Version (2 Timothy 1:9; 2 Peter 3:18). "Eternity" is a translation of the Greek word "aion." "Aion," translated "age," "world," "ever," and "forever," appears 126 times in the New Testament. It refers to a definite period called an "age" or "time," and it is in contrast with "kosmos" that refers to "people" or "space." Therefore, eternity is duration of time whether endless or limited. We are living in a period, an age. This age will end, and we will enter into an endless age.

We must properly understand the word "eternal." "Eternal" is most often translated from the Greek word "aionios," a form of the word "aion," speaking of the entirety of an age. This definition is true whether the new age ends or is endless in time. Paul said, **"While we do not look at the things which are seen, but at the things which are not seen. For the things which are seen** *are temporary* (proskairos*), but the things which are not seen are eternal* (aionios)*"* (2 Corinthians 4:18). The things that we see do not last the duration of this age (aion), but the unseen things last the duration of the eternal age (aionios).

When the Greek words "aionios" and "zoe" are combined, the translation is *"eternal life"* (John 3:16). The merging of Jesus and the believer generates eternal life, a focus more on the quality of life in the believer than the duration. This life is more than its duration, and is vastly different from the natural life of man because God's life generates the believer. John declared that life is present in the believer during the present age (aion). Jesus said, *"Most assuredly, I say to you, he who hears My word and believes in Him who sent Me has everlasting life, and shall not come into judgment, but has passed from death into life"* (John 5:24). In Jesus' high priestly prayer, He cried, *"And this is eternal life, that they may know You, the only true God, and Jesus Christ whom You have sent"* (John 17:3).

With this understanding of eternity, let us look at our passage. In the TONE of Jesus' severity, He makes a primary assumption. He did not need to explain it to those listening because they all understood. Jesus assumes everyone lives forever! All six illustrations (Matthew 5:21-48) prompted the truth of one statement, *"For I say to you, that unless your righteousness exceeds the righteousness of the scribes and Pharisees, you will by no means enter the kingdom of heaven"* (Matthew 5:20). According to the understanding and teachings of *"those of old,"* this would be impossible. From the legalistic approach of relationship with God, no one could dedicate themselves more than the scribes and Pharisees. But in the New Covenant the law is fulfilled in relationship. Our helplessness is filled with His presence; the empowerment for living happens on a new level.

How does this relate to our sexuality? *"Those of old"* viewed their sexuality as a body drive. Sin was involved only when the boundary placed on that drive was violated. A person must not go beyond the limit of satisfying that drive, *"You shall not commit adultery."* A passionate Jesus tried to explain that this problem is greater than breaking a rule. Sexuality is an issue of the heart. This means the heart, which you are, is expressed through your sexuality. If lust is involved in your looking, it is because you have self-centered sexuality in your heart, and adultery is present in the nature of your sexuality rather than the activity. What adultery is in the physical, self-centered sexuality is in the spiritual. Because the problem is the self-sourcing nature of the heart, the adultery of the heart may be expressed in the way you walk, talk, dress, approach life, or look at those of the opposite gender. Because you are an eternal being, this expression of who you are will exist forever.

Jesus' logic was simple and indisputable. Because you will live forever beyond this age and in the age that never ends, you would be better to be without a right eye or a right hand in this short age than to be constantly destroyed by self-centered sexuality in the age to come. The logic of His statement depends on the fact that everyone is going to live forever! To the Jews who were plotting to kill Him, Jesus said, *"Do not marvel at this; for the hour is coming in which all who are in the graves will hear His voice and come forth — those who have done good, to the resurrection of life, and those who have done evil, to the resurrection of condemnation"* (John 5:28-29). The righteous and the unrighteous live forever. Endless life is never the issue of the Scriptures. Everyone lives forever. The eternal age is not the continuation of life but the quality of life.

The continuation of life forever is a major issue! If a person makes careful plans for retirement, will he or she not more carefully plan for the eternal days of the age to come? Thoughts of how will I live, what if I am sick, or what resources will I need compel me to prepare for when we become senior adults. How much more does the eternal age demand our preparation? You and I are going to live forever!

Jesus taught the endless age, but He also proved the endless age by His resurrection. Some in the early Church who were concerned about their loved ones who died before them. They were expecting Jesus to return immediately the second time. However, when He did not, some of them died. Paul declared the continual message of the early Church as, *"Christ is preached that He has been raised from the dead"* (1 Corinthians 15:12). If so, why would anyone among us propose there is no resurrection of the dead? The logic is that if there is no resurrection of the dead then Jesus is not raised from the dead. If He is not raised from the dead, we are liars, and our preaching and our faith are empty (1 Corinthians 15:14-15).

The Pharisees were the force behind the crucifixion of Jesus. But the Book of Acts records that the Sadducees were the force of the persecution of the early Church. The message of the early Church was the resurrection of Jesus from the dead. If you embraced this resurrection that meant there is a resurrection from the dead and life beyond this short age. When being judged by the council, Paul proclaimed, *"Men and brethren, I am a Pharisee, the son of a Pharisee; concerning the hope and resurrection of the dead I am being judged!"* (Acts 23:6). This split the council because the Pharisees embraced the resurrection of the dead but the Sadducees did not. If you acknowledge the resurrection of Jesus, you must acknowledge the resurrection of every person. Everyone will live forever in the endless age to come.

This brings us to another conclusion of Jesus in our passage, the reality of TWICE. According to Jesus, there are only two destinations in which one may dwell in the coming endless age. We must continually remember that Jesus does not condemn or threaten. In our passage Jesus' approach is one of compassion and concern. Immediately after the Sermon on the Mount, Jesus went with His disciples to the cities and villages. *"But when He saw the multitudes, He was moved with compassion for them, because they were weary and scattered, like sheep having no shepherd"* (Matthew 9:36-37). He saw them under the weight of the leadership of *"those of old."* The burden of legalism was crushing them. He viewed them as they made their way to destruction with no shepherd, and He pleaded with them in the Sermon on the Mount.

In the first two illustrations, Jesus highlighted hell. In discussing the incarnation of Jesus, the Hebrew writer declared Jesus' victory over death. Through death He destroyed the one who had the power over death. In this context the writer declared, *"For indeed He does not give aid to angels, but He does give aid to the seed of Abraham"* (Hebrews 2:16-17). When the angels rebelled against God, their destruction was determined. God made no attempt to redeem or forgive them. However, when mankind sinned, God spared not His Son! The resource of the Trinity God focused on restoring us! This is why Jesus said in the parables of judgment, *"Then He will also say to those on the left hand, 'Depart from Me, you cursed, into the everlasting fire prepared for the devil and his angels'"* (Matthew 25:41-42). Hell was not prepared for man! Redemption was intended for man!

Jesus gave a further description of hell in the parables of judgment. *"And these will go away into everlasting punishment, but the righteous into eternal life"* (Matthew 25:46). The Greek word for *"everlasting"* is "aionios," describing the time of the endless age to come. We must properly understand the word *"punishment."* Two Greek words are translated "punishment," "timoria" and "kolasis." They may not differ in what the person being punished experiences, but they vastly differ in motive or intent of the one responsible for the punishment.

"Timoria" comes from classical Greek; it carries the predominant thought of the vindictive character of the punishment. This kind of punishment satisfies the inflictor's sense of outraged justice in defending his honor or that of the violated law. "Kolasis" is the Greek word used here (Matthew 25:46). It conveys the notion of punishment for the correction and bettering of the offender, but when "aionios" (everlasting) is included, it equals *"hell."* This is a final punishment from which we cannot return. However, there remains an important distinction between these two Greek words. In "kolasis" the relationship of the punishment is to the one being punished, and in "timoria" the relationship is to the punisher. In other words, the punishment of *"hell"* is not something forced on an individual because God is offended. The punishment is a direct result of the individual's choice; they embrace the punishment as a part of their lifestyle and choice.

The place of man's eternity was the intent of Jesus throughout the Sermon on the Mount. He highlighted the two possibilities of the endless age to come. As He closed the Sermon on the Mount, He spoke of those who proclaimed what they did in His name. He *"will declare to them, 'I never knew you; depart from Me, you who practice lawlessness!'"* (Matthew 7:23). These individuals had no relationship with Jesus, but they did have relationship with their lawlessness; thus, they will experience the consequences of this relationship. This relationship is the *"hell"* of our passage (Matthew 5:29-30).

We must not miss the TIMING of Jesus' conclusion. Jesus proposed that everyone lives forever in the endless age to come with the option of dwelling in one of two places. The one being emphasized in our passage is *"hell."* This place is not the result of the vindictive desire of Jesus but is the result of a person's choice. The choice we make in this age of time will determine our destination in the endless age to follow. The subject we are discussing is sexuality. Achievement of the standard of *"those of old"* will not suffice for the New Covenant, the Kingdom of Heaven. Jesus makes this plain with His challenge of a righteousness exceeding the righteousness of the scribes and Pharisees (Matthew 5:20). The choice is about embracing (mourning) our helplessness (poor in spirit). If this does not happen, we will remain self-sourced in our hearts, which will permeate our expression of sexuality including our viewpoint (looks).

If self-sourcing is maintained in this "time age," you will cross into the endless age with the focus of the condition you have maintained. Whether the crossing is death or Jesus' second coming, you will maintain the self-centered focus of your sexuality. Death does not save you; it is the blood of Jesus that transforms your inner heart. The focus of your life going into death is the focus of your life coming out of death into the endless age. Death does not afford you the option of change!

Involved in self-centeredness is the continual expansion of the focus. Even in this life, the self-centered focus in our sexuality cannot be limited or even maintained at a minimum because it is continually expanding. What satisfied the lust of your inner heart yesterday does not satisfy it today. The need is like a growing cancer that devours your life. When you view this from the perspective of the endless age, the raging lust of the inner heart filled with self-centeredness expands for unlimited ages to destroy all decency, morality, and relationship. You are warped, twisted, and completely dominated by your self-centered lust that cannot be satisfied. You have embraced your *"hell."*

Jesus cried, "Whatever is necessary to experience the Kingdom of Heaven, do it!" No self-centeredness can be tolerated! The inner self-centered heart must not be protected or pampered; pride must be radically exposed, and helplessness must be embraced. In this short age, there is no self-centered satisfaction worth the destruction of your self-centeredness in the endless age to come. This is a call to embrace Jesus!

12

PHYSICAL ETERNITY

MATTHEW 5:29-30

"If your right eye causes you to sin, pluck it out and cast it from you; for it is more profitable for you that one of your members perish than for your whole body to be cast into hell. And if your right hand causes you to sin, cut it off and cast it from you; for it is more profitable for you that one of your members perish, than for your whole body to be cast into hell" (Matthew 5: 29-30).

Many subjects were ignored in my religious training. I am not sure that the choice to ignore certain subjects was purposeful or the focus was on other important issues, but the result of this ignorance was assumptions. The knowledge of the things we talked about filtered into those areas we did not discuss. This caused me to assume many things that contradicted each other but were still accepted. Because we never spoke of these assumptions, there was never any correction.

One of these subjects was the extension of time into eternity. I understood from my training that Christians would live forever. Non-Christians would dwell in hell, but I was never told that they would live forever. We never discussed the reality of everyone living forever and being resurrected from the dead (John 5:29). Although living forever is a benefit for the Christian, the quality of that forever life is the ultimate experience. As we have discovered in these studies, everyone lives forever; everyone will be raised from the dead.

In what state will I dwell in my eternal life? I fear in our assumptions we have viewed the physical body as negative and an instrument of temptation because it is under the curse of sin. The deeds of sin that require physical action are directly connected to the physical. Even the sins of the spirit demonstrate themselves in the physical body. The limitation of the physical body such as sickness, tiredness, weakness, and pain contribute to the negative view. It becomes easy to assume that my eternal state will not have limitations of a body, but this assumption is wrong! In the context of a human body, Adam lived in intimacy with God before he sinned. God viewed His creation of Adam's physical being as good (Genesis 1:31).

Listen to the TONE of our passage. The presence of the physical body is unmistakable. Jesus referred to various parts of the body in the present and the *"whole body"* in the eternal. He did not reference our soul, spirit, or mind dwelling in hell. The issue is the *"whole body"* (holos soma). To understand the significance of Jesus' statement, we must investigate the Greek word "soma," translated *"body."* Its use in the New Testament is covered in four basic ideas.

One thought is "the complete person." "Soma" expresses the identity of the whole person as an entity before God, the inner person and the physical form. Paul challenged us, *"I beseech you therefore, brethren, by the mercies of God, that you present your bodies* (soma) *a living sacrifice, holy, acceptable to God, which is your reasonable service"* (Romans 12:1). In regard to Paul's personal dedication to Jesus, he said, *"But I discipline my body* (soma) *and bring it into subjection, lest, when I have preached to others, I myself should become disqualified"* (1 Corinthians 9:27).

We must align our perspective of "body" (soma) with the incarnation. The writers of the New Testament accepted the humanity of Jesus (Romans 7:4). There are many references to His physical body at the time of His death (Matthew 27:58; Luke 24:3, 23; John 19:38, 40; 20:12). The incarnation is God's ultimate endorsement of the physical body (Matthew 1:20-25; Luke 1:26-35; Romans 1:3; Galatians 4:4; 1 Timothy 3:16; 1 John 4:2-3). Jesus' body was the location of humanity's redemption. This redemption demanded that the Word become flesh and dwell among us (John 1:14). Jesus' body was the temple of God's glory and the sacrificial offering for the sins of a world! Even His resurrection demanded a physical body (to be discussed later).

In light of the integration of body and spirit, "soma" does not mean something external to man himself. The body is not something man has but something he is! Although we recognize the distinction between the spiritual and physical existence of man, he cannot be without the unity of the two. Even in our passage Jesus points to this interworking. Adultery, a physical act, happens in the spiritual realm of the heart that controls the viewpoint of the *"looks"* of the physical eye. If it is the right eye or the right hand that causes you to sin, it should be cut off and thrown away. However, the right eye or the right hand is not the cause the sin. Sin comes from the spiritual heart. The merging of the spiritual and physical is the core consideration of redemption.

Another consideration of "soma" is "the context of the person." The body is the location or dwelling place of the spiritual man, where the sourcing of the Spirit of Jesus can be seen. The spiritual man expresses the sourcing of the Spirit of Jesus through his body. The body is the arena in which he practices his faith (invoking the activity of the Second Party). Paul cried, *"Or do you not know that your body is the temple of the Holy Spirit who is in you"* (1 Corinthians 6:19). Through the sourcing of the indwelt Spirit, the body becomes the expression of the Kingdom relationship in the present.

Man cannot be himself unless the body and spirit coordinate and function as a whole through the sourcing of the Spirit of Jesus. The body merges with the spirit providing the agency for expression. Neither the body nor the spirit takes precedence over the other because each benefits the other. Thus, the body is the platform for the expression of the whole person. What value is the brain without the hands to act out its thoughts? What value is the love filled heart without arms to embrace? What value is a song in the inner soul without the voice to declare it? The body is the context through which a person gives expression.

Our passage declares this truth. While *"those of old"* considered their sexuality an animal body drive to be controlled, Jesus understood that the sexuality expressed through the body is a product of the heart. Paul said, *"Flee sexual immorality. Every sin that a man does is outside the body, but he who commits sexual immorality sins against his own body"* (1 Corinthians 6:18). When a man murders, he sins against his brother, but sexual sins are the destruction of self! In sexual sin we war against our being! That is why Paul admonished, *"So husbands ought to love their own wives as their own bodies; he who loves his wife loves himself"* (Ephesians 5:28).

"Soma" is also the "combination of the person." This is the reality of the resurrection because "soma" was the vehicle of the resurrection. The New Testament does not speak of the soul or the nonmaterial aspect of man's existence being resurrected. The consistent focus is on the resurrection of the physical body. *"But if the Spirit of Him who raised Jesus from the dead dwells in you, He who raised Christ from the dead will also give life to your mortal bodies through His Spirit who dwells in you"* (Romans 8:11). The total man is both spirit and physical body!

Jesus linked sexuality with the inner spirit of man, *"his heart"* (Matthew 5:28), but when considering eternity, the concern is the physical body (Matthew 5:29-30). Lust in the spirit of man bears consequences in the physical body. The spirit of man and the physical body merge until either one can represent both. They are so intimately combined that each participates in the function of the other. The damnable doctrine of separating the spiritual from the physical is never suggested. Jesus said that sexuality is not exclusively a matter of the inner spirit, but it determines what the physical eye sees.

The fourth use of "soma" is the "commitment of the

person." The physical body becomes the platform for spiritual testing and the demonstration of the inner spirit's commitment. Jesus called our inner spiritual condition, *"poor in spirit"* (Matthew 5:3). The inner spirit is helpless, and when it tries to control the body, the physical dominates and dictates the expression of the inner being through the flesh. Therefore, Paul said, *"For those who live according to the flesh set their minds on the things of the flesh, but those who live according to the Spirit, the things of the Spirit"* (Romans 8:5). Therefore, Jesus taught that sexuality gives expression to the spirit that controls it. If we are filled with self-centeredness, the physical body will serve the self-sourced flesh. If the Spirit of Jesus controls us, the body will respond to the discipline of the Spirit. Everyone is surrendered either to self-sourcing or to the sourcing of Jesus. The physical body reveals the surrender! Thus, the physical body and its demonstration becomes a key factor in our eternal state!

Jesus used this emphasis TWICE in our passage. The dual statement concerning the body being cast into hell is significant, but we could logically question it. Throughout the Sermon on the Mount, He moved us from an external view to an internal view. Regarding physical murder, He said anger is spiritual murder and is the real issue! In sexuality the issue is the inner heart. The inner spirit controls what we see when looking. We would expect the inner heart or spirit of man to be cast into hell, but in this passage Jesus highlights the *"whole body."*

Jesus did not want us to miss the truth of His statement. It would be easy to develop a religion that separates the outward activity of the body from the spirit of the heart. Many New Testament epistles deal with this kind of

"Gnosticism," a separation between the spirit of man and the physical body. Gnosticism believes the flesh of man is evil and will never be redeemed. The Gnostics taught that the flesh of man could continue in lust and sinful sexuality while the spirit of man could be pure and holy and could not be defiled regardless of the gross evil of the flesh. Their teaching said the spirit of man could go its way in waves of holiness and purity but the body was free to indulge its fleshly desires. This teaching is never the message of the Bible!

Jesus supported the Old Testament concept of man's creation, a dichotomy in structure. *"And the Lord God formed man of the dust of the ground, and breathed into his nostrils the breath of life; and man became a living being"* (Genesis 2:7). The Hebrew word "yatsar," translated *"formed,"* describes how the hands of God fashioned man. "Yatsar" is the image of the potter skillfully working with clay to form his mind's design. God creatively formed man's physical body, but that did not end His involvement. He *"breathed"* into man the *"breath of life."* God shared or imparted His spirit and life into man, and in this union of body and spirit, man became a *"living being."* Man was not a living being until God gave him a body and added His spirit. Man is a union of body and spirit.

You are unique in personality and physical structure. Your fingerprints are different from all others; your DNA is yours alone. God created your physical structure to match your spirit. You are a matched set! Jesus died to redeem not only your spirit but also your body (Romans 8:23). In our passage Jesus interlocks the relationship of man's heart with his physical body. When adultery reigns in the self-centered heart, it expresses itself through the lustful looking of the physical eye. The entire body participates in the desires of the self-centered heart; therefore, hell is for the whole being, which includes the physical.

Currently we understand that the spiritual heart and the physical body are interlocked. We live this experience daily, the truth of TIMING. We display through physical interaction what is happening in our spiritual hearts. Our physical circumstances can cause anxiety in our hearts, which pressurizes our bodies with emotional stress and sometimes creates physical illnesses.

When man's heart is filled with self-centered sexuality the body drives respond to fulfill that desire. Jesus said that lust is not a product of our body's sexual drive but is a product of the self-centered heart dictating its desires. That self-centered heart seeks to intensify, focuses, and control the natural sexual desire of the body. *"Those of old"* wanted to attack the problem with a commandment, an effort to control the body drive. Jesus warned that the issue is not the sexual body drive but the self-centeredness of the heart. This issue is the predicament of our present age.

We must not think that the connection between the inner heart and the physical body is true only for our days on Earth. This problem extends into eternity! There is the mistaken idea is that death will cure the sinful desires that flow from the heart to the body and at death our sinful desire will magically disappear, freeing us. But death is not our savior; Jesus is our Savior. We must embrace our helplessness, *"poor in spirit."* When we embrace our helplessness in mourning grief, Jesus can enter our hearts and save us from ourselves. This entrance has to happen in the present age.

Can you imagine passing from this life into the next with the self-centered heart continuing to demand satisfaction from the physical body? The dominant characteristic of self-centeredness is lack of satisfaction. That which satisfies you today will need to increase tomorrow. If two pills satisfy the addict today, he will need four pills tomorrow for the same effect, and in a month he will need thirty. It should terrify us to think about what self-centeredness will demand of us in the millions of years to come. That demand of the growing and increasing rage is the state of hell. The body will not be able to keep up with the demanded level of satisfaction from the self-centered heart. Self-centeredness destroys the life of the living being, body and spirit.

The cry of Jesus warns us to deal with whatever "causes us to sin" in light of eternity. Eternity's consequences are extreme! Self-centeredness is the core issue of the heart, and we must confront it with severity because it is the most difficult issue of my life! *"Pluck it out and cast it from you." "Cut it off and cast it from you."* We must take sides with Jesus against our self-centeredness. He has already won the victory for us!

13

PLACE OF THE EFFECTS

MATTHEW 5:29-30

"If your right eye causes you to sin, pluck it out and cast it from you; for it is more profitable for you that one of your members perish than for your whole body to be cast into hell. And if your right hand causes you to sin, cut it off and cast it from you; for it is more profitable for you that one of your members perish, than for your whole body to be cast into hell" (Matthew 5: 29-30).

Maintaining the perspective or idea of our passage is important (Matthew 5:27-30). We are thrust into a new level of living when our helpless being merges with Jesus' empowering Person in the new Kingdom relationship. As a Kingdom person, we experience a righteousness that exceeds that of the scribes and Pharisees (Matthew 5:20). In the Sermon on the Mount, Jesus gives six illustrations of this righteousness, of which our passage is the second.

"Those of old" saw their sexuality as a body appetite

they needed to control. The best they could do was to follow the standard, *"You shall not commit adultery"* (Matthew 5:27). In the Kingdom relationship, the "heart" is the issue. The "heart" determines the view of the eye, the stride of the walk, the style of the dress, and the approach to life. In other words, sexuality permeates the expression of the life; this expression is determined by the nature of the heart. When self-centeredness controls the heart, the expression of masculinity or femininity is selfish. At the conclusion of Jesus' illustration He becomes serious and forceful, using extreme language (Matthew 5:29-30).

Jesus uses two identical statements to express three ideas. One is the ESSENTIALITY of Spirit-sourced sexuality. A person's spiritual life has value above all else! We must eliminate from our sexuality anything self-centered that causes stumbling. This elimination does not come through forgiveness but through crucifixion. We must cut it off and cast it from us. Jesus' second proposal brings into focus the ETERNALNESS of our physical body. The intimate link of my spiritual with my physical goes far beyond the limits of time. This link is an eternal experience. The physical body is an intricate element of the eternal being of every individual. Jesus' third consideration is the EFFECTS of the self-sourced sexuality in life. To understand the seriousness of self-sourced sexuality, we must consider the consequences. In our present study, the place of the effects is the first of three in an investigation of the effects of self-sourcing.

We will begin with the TONE of the place. If you are seeking truth, it is unwise to be dogmatic about the Old Testament view of eternity. That view was so vague that the Sadducees dismissed it entirely. We are left to surmise only a surface understanding of the progression that brings us to our present state. The Old Testament presented to us a place called "Sheol." This Hebrew word appears in the Old Testament sixty-five times. "Sheol" is translated "grave" thirty-one times (Genesis 37:35; 42:38; 44:29, 31; 1 Samuel 2:6, etc.). The inhabitants of "Sheol" were "the congregation of the dead" (Proverbs 21:16), the abode of the wicked (Numbers 16:33; Job 24:19, Psalms 9:17; 31:17, etc.), and of the good (Psalms 16:10; 30:3; 49:15, 86:13, etc.). "Sheol" is described as deep (Job 11:8), dark (Job 10:21-22), and with bars (Job 17:16) where the dead "go down" to it (Numbers 16:30-33; Ezekiel 31:15-17). "Sheol" was an intermediate and shadowy place where souls went after earthly death.

"Sheol" contained two compartments. The upper chamber was called "paradise." Jesus assured the thief on the cross that he would be with Him in "Paradise" (Luke 23:43). *"Paradise"* was not a promise for a future, but a promise fulfilled at his death, a place for the abode of the dead who were righteous. The lower compartment was called "Hades," not to be confused with "hell," and it was an intermediate dwelling place for the wicked. Neither the righteous nor unrighteous reached their final dwelling place in "Sheol."

Again we must emphasize the vast opinions on the dwelling places after earthly death. The Old Testament view is vague about eternity and equally vague on what the death of Jesus accomplished in regard to "Sheol." Surely Jesus' entrance into the abode of the dead, burdened with our sin, and His experience of the resurrection power of the Father altered "Sheol" forever. From that point forward we are told of the New Testament concept of heaven and hell. Paul assured us that *"to be absent from the body and to be present with the Lord"* (2 Corinthians 5:8). We might conclude that Jesus entered into "Sheol" and in the power of His resurrection disassembled it. Heaven and hell were established through the judgment of His death on the cross. Jesus referred to His crucifixion as, *"the judgment of this world; now the ruler of this world will be cast out"* (John 12:31). We no longer need to abide in an intermediate place waiting for judgment because judgment took place at the cross. Our response to His death is the judgment of our lives, and we dwell in that judgment now. Eternal life or eternal death is already happening in us. Death does not bring us to judgment; death is a transition into a permanent dwelling place called "heaven" or "hell." The state of judgment in which we dwell now and will dwell at the time of death will continue forever.

In our passage Jesus expressed deep concern about sin in our hearts. When our sexuality is controlled by a heart ruled by self-sourcing, our lives give continual expression to sin. He presents His concern within the framework of a place called *"hell." "Hell"* is a translation of the Greek word "geenna," used twelve times in the New Testament. Outside of the Epistle of James (3:6), Jesus was the only one who used this word! In the New Testament Jesus said more about *"hell"* than any other biblical person.

When and where was Jesus compelled to address the issue of *"hell"*? He used *"hell"* nine times in speaking to His disciples, calling attention to their self-centeredness. In His final public message, Jesus used this word twice in reference to the self-centered scribes and Pharisees (Matthew 23:15, 33). All of these discussions were focused on self-sourcing religious people working within the context of religion.

Now with this understanding of Jesus' references to *"hell,"* let us consider our passage (Matthew 5:29-30). The Sermon on the Mount was the message Jesus designed for His disciples (Matthew 5:1-2). However, in the immediate context of our passage, He addressed the self-sourced approach of the religious leaders of Israel. The righteousness of the Kingdom person must exceed the righteousness of the scribes and Pharisees (Matthew 5:20). Concerning sexuality, the scribes' and Pharisees' hearts were sourced by their self-centeredness, which determined the expression of their sexuality. Their self-centered sexuality shaped their culture, religious rules, and the treatment of the opposite gender. Jesus discussed *"hell"* in connection only with this self-centeredness. If the demonic nature of self-centeredness creates a spiritual death, it can be described only in terms of *"hell."*

Knowing that Jesus spoke to His disciples and the self-sourced religious leaders of Israel about *"hell,"* let us contrast that with all the times He spoke to other sinners but did not speak about *"hell."* *"Then the scribes and Pharisees brought to Him a woman caught in adultery"* (John 8:3). The law demanded that she should be stoned, and they confronted Jesus to test Him. Jesus addressed the woman caught in the act and her accusers, but He never spoke of *"hell."* In the biblical encounters between Jesus and the wicked tax collectors, *"hell"* was never mentioned (Luke 19:1-10; Luke 5:27-32). Therefore, if we were to preach as Jesus did, we would preach only on *"hell"* to self-centered religious people. Jesus never used *"hell"* to frighten the sinful majority into responding to His message. He spoke of *"hell"* only to awaken those who received so much knowledge and light from God but used such revelation for their self-centeredness.

Now let us consider the TWICE of the place to discover the content of *"hell."* We have learned that the Greek word "geenna," translated *"hell"* (Matthew 5:22), is derived from the Hebrew expression, "Valley of Hinnom" (Joshua 15:8; Nehemiah 11:30). This valley lay to the south and southwest of Jerusalem. Topographically it provided the border between Judah and Benjamin (Joshua 15:8; 18:16) and the northern limit of the district occupied by the tribe of Judah after the captivity (Nehemiah 11:30), and it lay in front of the gate Harsith in Jerusalem (Jeremiah 19:2).

The "Valley of Hinnom" became a place of idolatrous and human sacrifices. These sacrifices were first offered by Ahaz and Manasseh who made their children to *"pass through the fire"* to Molech in this valley (2 Kings 16:3; 2 Kings 21:6; 2 Chronicles 28:3; 33:6). These sacrifices were probably made on the *"high places of Tophet which is in the Valley of the Son of Hinnom"* (Jeremiah 7:31). In order to put an end to these abominations, Josiah polluted it with human bones and other corruptions (2 Kings 23:10, 13, 14). But this worship to Molech was revived under Jehoiakim (Jeremiah 11:10-13; Ezekiel 20:30). Because of these idolatrous practices in the Valley of Hinnom, Jeremiah prophesied that one day it would be called the *"Valley of Slaughter"* (Jeremiah 7:32), and that they should, *"bury them in Tophet, till there be no place to bury"* (Jeremiah 19:11).

In New Testament days, the *"Valley of Slaughter"* became the garbage dump of Jerusalem. No other use was possible because of its defilement. A constant fire was burning the refuse. The stench of burning human flesh hovered over Jerusalem because the dead were often thrown into this valley. As Jesus spoke to the disciples or the leaders of Israel about "Geenna," they had a vivid picture of this place called *"hell."*

Many descriptive statements in the New Testament strengthen the physical imagery of the valley constantly burning refuse. Even the ungodly will be raised from the dead and will be given an eternal body that can endure the pain and agony of *"hell"* forever. Jesus cried, *"And do not fear those who kill the body but cannot kill the soul. But rather fear Him who is able to destroy both soul and body in hell"* (Matthew 10:28). The destruction includes the spiritual part of man and the physical body of man; it is not destruction in the absolute sense of annihilation but an eternal state of progressive pain and ruination.

Gehenna is as a fire. Jesus said, *"But whoever says, 'You fool!' shall be in danger of hell fire"* (Matthew 5:22). The words of Jesus in our passage (Matthew 5:29-30) are repeated in chapter eighteen (Matthew 18:8-9), with additional statements, *"to be cast into everlasting fire"* (Matthew 18:8), and *"to be cast into hell fire"* (Matthew 18:9). Mark also records this same statement. *"If your hand causes you to sin, cut it off. It is better for you to enter into life maimed, rather than having two hands, to go to hell, into the fire that shall never be quenched — where 'Their worm does not die and the fire is not quenched.'"* (Mark 9:43-44).

Mark also quotes Jesus saying this about the foot as well as the hand and eye (Mark 9:43-48). The same description is given three times, twice by Matthew and once by Mark. Jesus explains the Parable of the Tares in the Parables of the Kingdom. He said, *"The Son of Man will send out His angels, and they will gather out of His kingdom all things that offend, and those who practice lawlessness, and will cast them into the furnace of fire. There will be wailing and gnashing of teeth"* (Matthew 13:41-42). Jesus makes the same statement in the Parable of the Dragnet (Matthew 13:50). He used the imagery of, *"outer darkness; there will be weeping and gnashing of teeth"* in the Parable of the Wedding Feast (Matthew 22:13) and the Parable of the Talents (Matthew 25:30). The Book of Revelation often uses the imagery of *"cast alive into the lake of fire burning with brimstone"* (Revelation 19:20; 20:10, 14, 15; 21:8).

The Bible exhausts human language in its description of the horrible suffering and state of existence in hell. However, the same occurs in its description of the abundance of life found in heaven. How much of the language is literal or symbolic? For instance, is there physical fire experienced in hell? The contradictions in the descriptions point toward symbolic language. *"Outer darkness"* and the idea of burning *"fire"* seem opposite. Despite your conclusion on the matter, heaven is more glorious and hell is more terrible than human language can express! We must be careful not to let the materialistic mindset of our culture dominate our viewpoint of heaven or hell.

The results of this study must bring us to the important conclusion of the TIMING of the place. Finality is the emphasis of Jesus! The logic of His statements vibrates with the temporary of the present and the forever quality of eternity, *"hell."* In fact, as Jesus makes these two statements to the disciples seeking position, He emphasizes this fact. Again, He expresses the seriousness of the self-centered focus of their masculinity. He changed the word *"hell"* to *"everlasting fire"* (Matthew 18:8). *"Hell"* is forever, consisting of an endless time. There may be a beginning but there is no end.

If we conclude that "hell" is not to be the final dwelling place for our lives, then the consideration immediately becomes how to avoid this dwelling place. The answer is not found in the moment of physical death, which is not the solution. Many people have accepted the deception that physical death will change their attitude, spiritual condition, and character. All their bad habits will suddenly disappear; hatred and bitterness will vanish; inner stress and anxiety will no longer plague them. This conclusion may be a result of the belief that this world creates these problems for them, and they are not responsible. These ideas are a part of the deception of the enemy; do not be fooled!

In our passage Jesus addressed our sexuality. Adultery and lust are natural in this life that causes us to conclude that these things are a result of living in this world, and the next world will be different. Jesus boldly said this conclusion is false! Adultery and lust are a direct result of the heart's condition. If you die with this heart, you will dwell in another world with the same condition. Death is not the savior; Jesus is the only One who can change our hearts!

This brings us to the awareness of the importance of immediate inner change. If we do not want to go to the place of eternal death, we must not possess the condition of eternal death now! Hell is not a future experience but the beginning stage of this place that exists within the individual. Physical death is a door closing behind us, and it removes us from the possibility of any change of our inner condition. Whatever you and I are in our hearts when we physically die will be what we will be forever. Physical death is not the cure.

Is this not why Jesus desperately hounds us? John, the Apostle, consistently referred to Jesus as "the Light." John the Baptist was not the light, but he gave testimony to *"the Light."* He said that Jesus *"gives light to every man coming into the world"* (John 1:9). By every circumstance of your life, by every word spoken to you, and by the determined plan of God for your intervention, God is drawing you into His eternal life. If you remain in eternal death and dwell forever-in eternal hell, you will have to fight against the consistent revelation of truth from Jesus! Those dwelling in eternal hell will admit forever of their personal choice to do so. Today is the time of choice!

"Today, if you will hear His voice, do not harden your hearts as in the rebellion" (Hebrews 3:15).

"Today, if you will hear His voice, do not harden your hearts" (Hebrews 4:7).

14

PUNISHMENT OF THE EFFECT

MATTHEW 5:29-30

"If your right eye causes you to sin, pluck it out and cast it from you; for it is more profitable for you that one of your members perish than for your whole body to be cast into hell. And if your right hand causes you to sin, cut it off and cast it from you; for it is more profitable for you that one of your members perish, than for your whole body to be cast into hell" (Matthew 5: 29-30).

The Sermon on the Mount flows from a Divine attitude. Matthew was specific when he gave us the sequence of events to bring us to this presentation. *"In those days John the Baptist came preaching in the wilderness of Judea, and saying, 'Repent, for the kingdom of heaven is at hand!'"* (Matthew 3:1-2). John's call was to "give up a former thought to embrace a new thought." Although this involves confession of sins and turning from them, the impact of our response is that we give up the Old

Covenant (law-sourcing) to embrace the New Covenant (Spirit-sourcing). The Greek word "gar," translated *"for,"* is the reason for repentance. The Kingdom of Heaven is now present. We are not to repent so the Kingdom will come, but we repent because the Kingdom has come. Repentance is a response to an act of God on our behalf. The message contains no threat, warning, or ultimatum, only an urgent invitation. Any hint of warning is given to the self-centered leaders of Israel (Matthew 3:7-12).

Jesus was the first man to be filled with the Spirit (Matthew 3:16). The Spirit led Jesus into the wilderness temptation (Matthew 4:1-11) and gave Him victory over that temptation. The leaders of Israel put John the Baptist in prison at the same time Jesus began His Galilean ministry, attracting multitudes from every region (Matthew 4:25). Jesus, a Spirit-sourced Man, met the needs of thousands of hurting people, revealing His attitude of mercy, love, and concern!

The Sermon on the Mount is Jesus' manifesto on the Kingdom of God. His message begins with a blessing. The Beatitudes flow with Jesus' excited congratulation not condemnation (Matthew 5:3-12). The final Beatitude encourages this attitude amid persecution. Jesus does not consider hating those who persecute you a part of the Kingdom person. In fact, the function of the Kingdom person is one of *"salt"* and *"light"* (Matthew 5:13-16) with the absence of punishment or judgment. ***"Let your light so shine before men, that they may see your good works and glorify your Father in heaven"*** (Matthew 5:16). Letting your light shine demonstrates nothing negative, partial, or prejudiced.

Jesus presents Himself in a clear revelation of

"fulfillment." The negative of destruction, elimination, or brokenness is not in His destiny. This "fulfillment" produces righteousness beyond the limited love, judgment, and condemnation of the scribes and Pharisees (Matthew 5:17-20). Jesus provides six illustrations to prove this righteousness. *"You shall not murder"* is the focus of the first illustration. Not committing murder was a boundary for living of *"those of old."* They allowed judgment, ridicule, and hatred in contrast to the love, reconciliation, and respect of the Kingdom person. Jesus' second illustration concerns sexuality. *"Those of old"* established a boundary permitting everything except adultery, but the Kingdom person rejects this thought process! The sexuality of the Kingdom person does not use, abuse, or manipulate another for their satisfaction (Matthew 5:27-30). In Jesus third illustration, He says we should demonstrate this attitude of honor in marriage (Matthew 5:31-32) because a Kingdom person has integrity. This integrity eliminates the need of swearing by an oath because your word is your bond as Jesus presented in His fourth illustration (Matthew 5:33-37).

In His last two illustrations, Jesus said the intention of a Kingdom person is to never *"resist an evil person."* The Kingdom person's heart motive is one of giving, turning the other cheek, and going the extra mile (Matthew 5:38-42). The Kingdom person loves his enemies, blesses those who curse him, does well to those who hate him, and prays for those who spitefully use him. The Father's heart is the heart of the Kingdom person because they feel as the Father feels (Matthew 5:43-48).

The Kingdom has a TONE echoed by every statement of Jesus in the Sermon on the Mount! *"Those of old"* had their limits, but Jesus broke through and beyond these boundaries because there are no limits to love and its expression. By their attitude, *"those of old"* asked, "When have I loved enough?" "When have I turned the other cheek enough?" "When have I gone the second mile enough?" "When have I done enough good to those who hate me?" Jesus presented a limitless love and grace. He advocated continuous redemption without boundaries. He proposed that we are to have redemption without boundaries because in our helplessness we are filled with the nature of God. Was He telling us that God is like this?

Wait! If redemption without boundaries is true, what about our passage (Matthew 5:29-30)? Here Jesus proposed the punishment of *"hell."* Have we been wrong? Maybe *"hell"* is a reality but "punishment" is a misconception! Can there be an eternal death that dwells in an eternal hell, but it is not a punishment? Every parent should understand this! A child screams from the burning pain of touching a hot stove. He did not listen to his father's instruction to not touch the stove. Is the pain the punishment of the father or a natural consequence of the child's disobedience? Does the father delight in his child's suffering, or does he desire to bear his child's pain?

We must listen to the TONE of the Sermon on the Mount! If the "poor in Spirit" (helpless) are filled with the Father's nature, they will exhibit meekness, fullness, mercy, purity, peace, and rejoice in persecution. Where in the Sermon on the Mount does Jesus tell us to punish, hate, and seek the destruction of those who hurt us? We are the expression of the Father's nature! Does the Father not see us in the pain of our sin's consequences and want to take these consequences for us? Did He not do this in Christ on the cross? Has He not embraced all sin's results in its destruction? Did Jesus not go to hell for you? He has no desire to punish you! He wants only to save you!

Does this mean no one goes to hell? Obviously not! But it does mean that Jesus does not send you to hell. If anyone goes to hell, it is a consequence of his or her choice! I want to restate briefly from a previous study the biblical concept of "punishment." The two Greek words "timoria" and "kolasis," translated "punishment," do not differ in the experience of the person being punished, but they are vastly different in the motive or intent of the one responsible for the punishment.

"Timoria" comes from classical Greek, and it carries the predominant thought of the vindictive character of punishment. This kind of punishment satisfies the inflictor's sense of outraged justice in defending his honor or that of the violated law. "Kolasis" is the Greek word used in the parables of judgment. *"And these will go away into everlasting punishment, but the righteous into eternal life"* (Matthew 25:48), conveying the notion that punishment is for the correction or betterment of the offender. But when "aionios," translated *"everlasting,"* is included, it equals *"hell."* This is a final punishment from which you cannot return. However, there remains an important distinction between these two Greek words. In "kolasis" the relationship of the punishment is to the one being punished while in "timoria" the relationship is to the punisher. In other words, the punishment of *"hell"* is not something God forces on a person because He is offended. *"Hell"* is a direct result of the person's choice; they embrace the punishment as a part of their lifestyle and choice.

In the Sermon on the Mount, it was Jesus' intent to highlight the possibilities of heaven and hell for the endless age to come. As he closed the Sermon on the Mount, He spoke of those who proclaimed to prophesy, cast out demons, and do many wonders in His name. *"And then I will declare to them, 'I never knew you; depart from Me, you who practice lawlessness!'"* (Matthew 7:23). These people had no relationship with Jesus, but they did have relationship with their lawlessness. Therefore they will suffer the consequences of their choices. One consequence is the *"hell"* of our passage (Matthew 5:29-30). Listen to the tone of the Sermon on the Mount. If the Father's nature will not allow us to condemn, destroy, and hate, how can the Father have these vices? If the Father's nature causes us to love, forgive, and express mercy, can the Father damn, condemn, and destroy? Does He require more from us that He does from Himself? Are we not the expression of His heart?

It amazes me how often this tone appears in the biblical references to eternal death giving contrast between eternal life and eternal death. Paul said, *"For the wages of sin is death, but the gift of God is eternal life in Christ Jesus our Lord"* (Romans 6:23). The contrast is not between eternal life and eternal death but between *"wages"* and *"gift."* Eternal death does not come from God; eternal death is man's choice. We understand and participate in the economy of *"wages,"* because we deserve, earn and merit wages for our work. Our wages are not a result of revenge, anger, or punishment. Although our wages may come from an employer, we do not posture ourselves in the position of deserving them. We do not receive our paycheck then proclaim, "The boss is punishing me!" How is God pictured in this passage? He is the gracious, loving, and merciful one giving gifts! He did not select some to receive gifts and not others. He presents the gift to every person, but some stubbornly collect the wages they have earned while God offers His gift.

In the Parables of the Kingdom (Matthew 13), Jesus uses the imagery of farming. In the Parables of the Wheat and the Tares (Matthew 13:24-30), the climax of the story is the harvest. The good seed and the evil seed grow together in the world. The servants are upset over the conditions and desire to uproot the tares, but the owner is not, wisely instructing the servants to wait for the harvest. Tares will be gathered and burned at the harvest. This outcome is not a matter of anger, revenge, or punishment. Poisonous tares are worthless, making the proper action their destruction. This destruction is not a punishment but a natural conclusion of the harvest.

Jesus proposes the same idea TWICE in our passage (Matthew 5:29-30). It is important to know that the word *"cast"* appears twice in each statement and four times in the passage. The Greek word "ballo," translated *"cast,"* means "to drive out, expel, or throw away." This casting relates directly to sin. Jesus encourages us to find what causes us to sin and deal severely with it. We are not to pamper, save or coddle the instrument of sin. Sin must be so hideous in our sight that we "ballo" it from our lives. The word *"cast"* is in the active voice, meaning the subject of the imperative is responsible for the action of casting. The subject is you and I; we are responsible for throwing away the instrument that causes us to stumble.

Jesus uses the word *"cast"* again in the same sentence. He relates it to sin and the consequences of going to *"hell."* However, it is in the passive voice, meaning the subject (body) receives the action of the verb. In other words, you and I are not responsible for throwing ourselves into *"hell,"* but we receive *"hell"* as a consequence of our sin.

Jesus is logical in His approach to the subject of God's slightest involvement. He never said that God would punish us, or *"cast* (us) *into hell."* This act is a result of the destructive sin in our lives because of what we tolerate. If we do not severely confront whatever causes us to sin, sin will dominate our lives, and the end result of sin is *"hell."*

"Hell" is a reality. We never want to undermine its severity. We are not tying to lessen the destruction, lighten the suffering, or devalue the terrible fate of hell. But we do want to carefully examine the heart motive of God, who either causes or allows everything. His motive is one of love and deep concern. There is no hatred, bitterness, or anger in the heart of God for the sinner. However, there are consequences for choices we make. Although many may go to *"hell,"* it is not God's desire that any perish (2 Peter 3:9). *"Hell"* is a consequence and not a punishment!

In light of this truth about *"hell,"* we need to consider the TIMING. Jesus indicates a progression although it is not dominate. He contrasts this progression with the approach of *"those of old."* Their legalistic approach to *"You shall not commit adultery"* is a stagnant matter; you either do or you do not. However, Jesus spoke of an attitude of the heart (self-centeredness) controlling your sexuality, with the possibility of various degrees and intensity. What controls your heart begins to control your perspective. Your perspective begins to control the mannerisms, jokes, your approach to the opposite gender, and your attitude. Life becomes more controlled by your self-centered sexuality. *"Hell"* is the end of this progression? Sin will not rest until it brings destruction.

Jesus was persistent in presenting this progression though out His parables. The imagery of farming, seeds, and harvest offer this concept. This progression is not isolated to sin in the life of those who are evil, but is also present in the righteousness of the good seeds. In the Parable of the Wheat and the Tares, the owner discovers the tares and will not allow the servants to gather them. As the tares begin to show their presence among the wheat, any attempt to gather the tares will uproot the wheat as well. The owner's instructions are to, ***"Let both grow together until the harvest"*** (Matthew 13:30). Through the growth progression, the tares can be easily distinguished from the wheat.

Eternal death is not a condition to be experienced only in *"hell."* We experience eternal death when we are separated from God. Self-centeredness fills us because we lack His presence. Self-centeredness seems to be beneficial but consistently destroys everything it touches. Relationships are destroyed; peace and security change to anxiety and frustration when self does not achieve its goal. This spiritual death devours the person daily until death. Death is a moment of transition into a permanent state of separation from God. The person is released to a consistent and everlasting destruction of the self-centeredness he or she so desperately clung to in life. This state is called *"hell,"* and it is a continuation of what is experienced from the beginning and has come to full harvest.

No wonder Jesus used severe language. He urges us to do whatever it takes to break this cycle of self-centeredness. We must step out of eternal death and into eternal life in this moment. There is no better time than now. Jesus is life!

15

PROGRESSION OF THE EFFECT

MATTHEW 5:29-30

"If your right eye causes you to sin, pluck it out and cast it from you; for it is more profitable for you that one of your members perish than for your whole body to be cast into hell. And if your right hand causes you to sin, cut it off and cast it from you; for it is more profitable for you that one of your members perish, than for your whole body to be cast into hell" (Matthew 5: 29-30).

This chapter concludes our study of these two verses. This compels me to summarize the concepts we have discovered. We will repeat many things we previously said, cementing deep in our hearts our search for the truth as Jesus reveals who He is in us! Jesus gave us three basic ideas in these verses. ESSENTIALITY is an emphasis on the necessity of dealing with self-centered sexuality. He speaks to us in severe language. If you have any regard for your life, you will not hesitate to encounter this issue.

The second idea is the ETERNALNESS of your destiny. Eternity for each of us involves endless years, but our greatest concern should be the quality of those years with respect to our physical bodies. The concluding idea centers on the EFFECTS of self-sourced sexuality.

Although we may understand the principle of "cause and effect," we do not seem to apply that understanding to the circumstances of our lives. Even when we have irrefutable evidence that links cancer and smoking, many have asked, "Why do I have cancer?" The Greek word "dia" is often used in the Scriptures to highlight the "cause and effect." Many members of the Church of Corinth unworthily participated in the Lord's Supper. Paul said, *"For this reason many are weak and sick among you, and many sleep"* (1 Corinthians 11:30). Their sickness was the effect and a cause. In another place Paul described ungodly people, *"who exchanged the truth of God for the lie, and worshiped and served the creature rather than the Creator, who is blessed forever"* (Romans 1:25). Their actions caused a direct effect. *"For this reason God gave them up to vile passions"* (Romans 1:26).

The philosophical world debates the various theories of cause and effect, but none of that is necessary to our investigation. However, we can be certain of a link between cause and effect. They are so joined that the one is involved in the other with no way to divide them. When there is a definite relation between two events or state of affairs, the first is necessary for the second to occur.

The philosophers of old said there were four aspects of "cause." These are not four different "causes," but four elements that are necessary for forming "the cause." The first one is "The Formal Cause" and is the structure of the shape a thing takes. A blueprint is the cause of an airplane. The architectural drawings are the cause for the structure of a building. Jesus is the *"Word"* (John 1:1). The Greek word is "logos," an idea or thought. Jesus was the idea in the mind of God about mankind; He was the blueprint. In our passage (Matthew 5:29-30) sexuality is the blueprint in the creation of God. Every aspect of my life is shaped or determined by this blueprint. This blueprint determines the way I walk, think, react, approach life, and look at the opposite gender. *"Those of old"* missed this view. They thought their sexuality was a body appetite they had to control with a boundary rule, *"You shall not commit adultery."* The truth is that sexuality is a blueprint of the cause of your life, the important element of who you are!

Second, we have "The Material Cause." This element is the stuff of which a thing is made, determined by the blueprint. Sexuality is the internal nature acting itself out on the physical stage of my life. Sexuality is not a physical body drive that needs to be curbed or controlled, shifting the issue from my discipline of the physical drive to all expressions of my sexuality. My response when people hurt me is an expression of my internal nature. This "material" causes how I dress, walk, and my general attitude of life. Aristotle, the philosopher, treated this material cause as a relative term, relative to the structure that holds it together. For instance, the elements are the material cause of tissue while tissues are the material cause of the body organ. Body organs are the material cause of the living body. This thought means that the controlling nature of my life is the material cause of my sexuality. My sexuality is the material cause of my physical desire, and my desires become the expression of my life.

Sexuality is the blueprint for my life's formation. Through the nature of my sexuality, the material formed gives physical expression for my life. The third one is "The Efficient Cause." Although there may be a blueprint with the material fulfilling it, a builder created the blueprint. Jesus is our Creator. However, at this point is where the tragedy of sin enters the story. The demonic self-centered nature wooed man into independence from God. The blueprint of sexuality became tainted with self-satisfaction and focus. The self-centered nature shapes the material of sexuality for the fulfillment of pride. The self-centered nature dominates the expression of my sexuality for its fulfillment. The desires of the flesh become my passion under the domination of this builder.

"The Final Cause" is our fourth. Let us review! "The Formal Cause" is the blueprints of the airplane, and "The Material Cause" is the material that fulfills the blueprint. "The Efficient Cause" is the creator of the blueprints, but these three lead to purpose, "The Final Cause," the airplane is to transport people and cargo. We must now apply this to our passage (Matthew 5:29-30). Sexuality is God's blueprint for my life. The material fulfilling the blueprint and forming me is His nature! He is the Prime Mover of my life's expression, my sexuality. The purpose is the visualization of who He is! My world sees Jesus through my sexuality! But sin invaded my sexuality. It refocused my blueprint, reshaped the material of my sexuality, became the new creator of my sexuality's expression, and this self-centered nature came with a new purpose experienced in the effect of the cause!

In this section (Matthew 5:27-30) the TONE of the effect is destruction. Jesus is consistent in His Kingdom message. He crystallized this destruction in bold statements. *"If anyone desires to come after Me, let him deny himself, and take up his cross, and follow Me. For whoever desires to save his life will lose it, but whoever loses his life for My sake will find it"* (Matthew 16:24-25). When people focus on themselves for self-gain, they produce an effect of destruction, and the nature of self-centeredness becomes the cause ending in the effect of destruction. Every area of life operates under this principle. The opposite is also true. When people focus on self-giving and self-sacrifice, they find the effect of growth and strengthening in their lives.

Who are the people you consider your best friends? They are the people you can depend on. They have your back, go out of their way to help, and support you with encouragement. Who are the people with whom no relationship is possible? They consistently use you for their benefit and enjoy your defeat. You are only an instrument to acquire their desire. Their self-centeredness destroys any chance of relationship.

Jesus applies this principle to our sexuality. If self-centeredness is at the *"heart"* of our lives, it will manifest itself through our sexuality. Because our sexuality encompasses every area of our living, self-centeredness will be the dominant expression of our lives. The effect of this expression is destruction in every area. For instance, my self-centered sexuality will determine the perspective of my "looking." The effect of this in my life is *"lust."* The Greek word "epithymeo," translated *"lust,"* is the same Greek word translated "covet." *"You shall not commit adultery"* is the seventh commandment of the Ten Commandments. *"You shall not covet your neighbor's house; you shall not covet your neighbor's wife, nor his male servant, nor his female servant, nor his ox, nor his donkey, nor anything that is your neighbor's"* (Exodus 20:17). The heart of the word is the idea of having. In other words, if I covet, lust after my neighbor's house, I desire to take it from him, claim it as mine, and have it for myself. If I were to achieve this desire in the physical realm, I would remove the possession from my neighbor and take it for myself, becoming a thief! In the spiritual world, I am stealing my neighbor's house.

Our sexuality is intended to be intimate, sharing in one flesh and knowing each other by giving to each other. Now my sexuality, driven by my self-centered nature, becomes stealing. By self-centered lusting in the spiritual world, I not only steal my neighbor's wife, but I also steal from the woman what is not rightfully mine, robbing from her what is not mine. I am not giving; I am taking. My nature becomes so self-centered that I have become a cancer devouring others for my benefit. I am a spiritual thief, which is destruction.

When self-centeredness rules in the marriage relationship, it cannot produce "one flesh." Intimacy and love are absent. Marriage is destroyed, and we become instruments used by each other for self-satisfaction. No wonder Jesus uses such strong language, calling us to the elimination of all self-centeredness because the effect is far too costly.

To give a clear picture of the destruction, Jesus gives His answer to it TWICE. He presents the two realms of existence in each statement. The present state in which we dwell is a period of choice. The prevenient grace of God is aggressively manifesting itself in and around us. The Spirit of Jesus' nature and the self-centered demonic nature are contrasted and visualized before us.

Jesus begins with, *"If your right eye causes you to sin, pluck it out and cast it from you"* (Matthew 5:29). Jesus' appeal is that we embrace the opportunity we have in the present. We live in the present moment of decision, the most convenient, painless, manageable, uncomplicated, and simple time to deal with our self-centeredness. However, your pride will proclaim the opposite. Your circumstances will propose that leaving your self-centeredness is impossible. But the truth is clear; there will never be an easier time to surrender self to Jesus' nature. Your life is in an hourly progression. You establish patterns in each moment, and your heart is governed by your self-centered principles, collecting around you the things that cater to your self-centeredness. Now is the time to break free in Jesus!

But Jesus emphasis is not just on the present moments. He says, *"for it is more profitable for you that one of your members perish, than for your whole body to be cast into hell"* (Matthew 5:29). Our present moment of decision will not last. The effect of our self-centered sexuality casts its influence on all our relationships, mannerisms, and involvements, and that effect is long range! We cannot make decisions or corrections to our lifestyle in our final dwelling place because truth will not be heard. Darkness will be total. The self-centered cause of this hour not only affects the circumstances of your present life, but it also determines your eternal dwelling place.

Jesus told the story about a certain rich man. He described the man's fine apparel and how he, *"fared sumptuously every day"* (Luke 16:19). He compared this rich man with the beggar named Lazarus who was covered in sores, laid at the gate daily, and ate the crumbs from the rich man's table. Each man lived in the present moments of decision and then died. The eternal state of each man's dwelling place was fixed. The rich man cried for change and relief but found none. The story is not about riches compared to poverty, but about self-centeredness versus self-giving. The selfishness of the rich man consumed him in this life and in eternal life. Self-centeredness is destructive in the present, and it will continue to be in the eternal state!

The proposition of Jesus is that what is going on in your life now will continue to grow in the eternal realm, which brings us to the consideration of the TIMING. We cannot say this too often. The effects of self-centeredness are not temporary. These effects will not pass away, and you cannot shake them from your life in death. The cause of a self-centered heart will bring effects that span the course of time into eternity. What you are becoming now is what you will be forever.

What you are in your inner heart, your nature, is in constant progression. The effects in your state of existence will not level or plateau but will become permanent, growing in greater control and expanding in desire. We do not begin with a life of deceit, but as one lie builds up another deception takes over. Whatever your addiction it grows and increases the desire in you. What once satisfied you does not satisfy you now but increases daily to a greater degree in you.

The ancient philosophers held three beliefs about causality to be indisputable: nothing comes from nothing; nothing can give what it does not itself possess; and a cause must have as much perfection or being as it effects. The *"looks"* that produce *"lust"* and results in *"adultery with her in his heart"* does not happen accidentally. Nothing comes from nothing. There is a cause and effect. Jesus calls us to confront the cause and not the effect. This is not an hour for reform or newly applied disciplines. Now is a moment for the transformation of the self-centered heart!

The self-centeredness we demonstrate in our daily expressions of sexuality does not come from a heart filled with the Spirit of Jesus. We cannot give what we do not possess. A self-centered heart does not evolve into expressing kindness, love, and holiness. Hate does not evolve into love, anger does not evolve into patience, and sinfulness does not evolve into purity. Jesus calls us to deal with who we are in our hearts.

There is a parallel between the status of the heart and the status of the life we express. Do not be abhorred by the selfish condition of your action without realizing that your heart is filled with the same condition. A cause must have as much perfection or being as it effects. Look carefully at your expressions, and realize you are seeing the condition of your heart. Do not view the best of your deeds, the one you parade for the applause of others as your best. You must take a close look at your worst secret moments, the ones you do not want anyone else to know about. Realize in repentance that these secret moments are what you really are in your heart.

Think of the terribleness of a self-centered hell forever.

That hell is the revelation of the self-centered heart reaping total destruction of the human life. Whatever you may think hell will be like in the physical, realize with clarity that this will be the state of your inner heart, the cause!

MARRIAGE

THE FULFILLMENT
OF THE KINGDOM

16

THE DIVORCE ISSUE

MATTHEW 5:31-32

"Furthermore it has been said, 'Whoever divorces his wife, let him give her a certificate of divorce.' But I say to you that whoever divorces his wife for any reason except sexual immorality causes her to commit adultery; and whoever marries a woman who is divorced commits adultery" (Matthew 5:31-32).

Jesus is far too brief in His instructions about marriage and divorce. What is the subject of these two verses? Is it "marriage" or "divorce?" Perhaps it is not about either! We reserve that discussion for another study. "Divorce" was a major cultural problem in Jesus' day, but I am not sure that is comforting to anyone. The Pharisees used this controversy in their attempt to discredit Jesus (Matthew 19:1-10). Two thousand years later we are still in that controversy with various problems of sexuality related to marriage increasing in their complexity. How you feel about these problems is for you to decide, and we encourage you to allow your conclusions to flow from your saturation in His Word and His presence!

The biblical background for marriage and divorce comes from the Old Testament culture where God made provision through Moses for divorce. Jesus was clear in his statement about God's motivation to provide for divorce. *"Moses, because of the hardness of your hearts, permitted you to divorce your wives, but from the beginning it was not so"* (Matthew 19:8). That is very plain! God never intended the option of divorce from the beginning or in the present day, but because of the evil in the heart of man, God made the provision in the laws of Deuteronomy. *"When a man takes a wife and marries her, and it happens that she finds no favor in his eyes because he has found some uncleanness in her, and he writes her a certificate of divorce, puts it in her hand, and sends her out of his house"* (Deuteronomy 24:1).

The "certificate of divorce" was a legal document to dismiss the marriage. Such a document would appear as follows:

On the day of the week A. in the month B. in the year C. from the beginning of the world, according to the common computation in the province of D, I, N. the son of N. by whatever name I am called, of the city E. with entire consent of mind, and without any compulsion, have divorced, dismissed, and expelled thee-thee, I say, M. the daughter of M. by whatever name thou art called, of the city E. who wast heretofore my wife: but now I have dismissed thee-thee, I say, M. the daughter of M. by whatever name thou art called, of the city E. so as to be free, and at thine own disposal, to marry whomsoever thou pleasest, without hinderance from anyone, from this day forever. Thou art therefore free for any man. Let this be thy bill of divorce from me, a writing of separation and expulsion, according to the law of Moses and Israel.

REUBEN, son of Jacob, Witness.

ELIEZAR, son of Gilead, Witness.[1]

We must understand this information through the Jewish culture of the New Testament. The husband paid a dowry to secure the right of marriage to his wife. Wives were considered the property of their husbands, and by Mosaic statutes women did not possess the right to dissolve the marriage. Only the husband had the privilege of giving a bill of divorce. Josephus (Jewish historian during New Testament days, a non-Christian) was of the opinion that the law did not permit women to divorce their husbands. He thought that Salome, sister of Herod the Great, was the first woman to put away her husband, though Herodias afterward dismissed her.

The right to divorce was not a major debate in Jesus' day because it was a common and acceptable practice. The heated discussions centered on the reason for divorce, focusing on the statement, *"some uncleanness in her."* During the time of the Gospel accounts, there were two schools of learning, Hillel and Shammai. The School of Hillel strongly disagreed with the School of Shammai. Hillel represented the liberal interpretation of the statement, *"some uncleanness in her,"* extending the cause to her burning or over salting his food. If the husband saw a woman whose appearance pleased him better than his wife, it was acceptable for him to divorce

---

1 • Adam Clarke's Commentary, Electronic Database. Copyright © 1996, 2003, 2005, 2006 by Biblesoft, Inc. All rights reserved.

her. The School of Shammai represented the conservative interpretation of the statement, limiting divorce to a moral delinquency in the woman, mainly adultery.

We cannot find anywhere in the Word of God where the act of divorce is pronounced as a sin. From the beginning God never intended that divorce be an option. Jesus moved into the region of Perea beyond the Jordan, the territory under the jurisdiction of Herod Antipas. The beheading of John the Baptist was the raging controversy in this area. The problem behind this controversy was the adulterous affair and divorce of Herod and Herodias. Herodias was Philip's wife, the brother of Herod (Matthew 14:3-12). The Pharisees, desiring to trap Jesus, approached Him before a multitude with the issue of divorce. Their question to Him was, *"Is it lawful for a man to divorce his wife for just any reason?"* (Matthew 19:3). Jesus reminded them of their Scriptures. He quoted the intent of God from the beginning, which was that there was no provision for divorce (Matthew 19:4-6). God hates divorce, does not want divorce, and never intended that we dissolve a marriage by divorce (Malachi 2:16).

Jesus' response caused the Pharisees to see an opportunity to accuse Him. Was Jesus contradicting the commandment of Moses? No! Moses did what God wanted, but,

"Moses, because of the hardness of your hearts, permitted you to divorce your wives, but from the beginning it was not so" (Matthew 19:8). God made the allowance of divorce because of the self-centeredness of man's heart. Although divorce may not be the primary intent and desire of God, it may not be voluntary disobedience against His known will for your life. The

overwhelming proof of this position is that while God hates divorce, He declared divorce against Israel, *"Then I saw that for all the causes for which backsliding Israel had committed adultery, I had put her away and given her a certificate of divorce; yet her treacherous sister Judah did not fear, but went and played the harlot also"* (Jeremiah 3:8).

Now we come to our passage (Matthew 5:31-32) where the issue is not "divorce" or "no divorce." Jesus does not address the sinfulness of divorce. He embraces the hurt and pain produced by the self-centeredness of the carnal nature. He is aware that sometimes divorce is necessary, which was also accepted by His culture. The issue for debate concerned the proper cause for divorce in that culture. Was the liberal approach of the School of Hillel correct? Can you get a divorce for just any reason such as burnt food or over-salted meat? Or is the conservative approach of the School of Shammai correct? Who is right? Jesus said, *"Furthermore it has been said, 'Whoever divorces his wife, let him give her a certificate of divorce'"* (Matthew 5:31).

How does Jesus answer the question? A major problem I have with Jesus is that He never stays with the subject I want to discuss. He does not address the question that I want answered. Jesus responds with, *"But I say to you that whoever divorces his wife for any reason except sexual immorality causes her to commit adultery; and whoever marries a woman who is divorced commits adultery"* (Matthew 5:32). It is easy to misread what Jesus said in our translation and in other interpretations of this verse. We are so focused on the question we want answered that the purpose of Jesus' statement is lost. Do we really want to know what Jesus said? Can we come with an open mind to the revelation of His Spirit?

I want to know when it is right for me to get a divorce? What is the proper basis for divorcing my spouse so I know that I am right and she or he is wrong? From Jesus' perspective the fact that we ask this question reveals we do not have the proper spiritual insight. Perhaps the crisis in your marriage does not warrant divorce, but that is not the issue. Whether I am right or wrong in seeking a divorce is not the issue either. If I focus on this question, I will miss the purpose for which God allowed this marriage crisis to happen in my life.

What is the truth concerning divorce from our passage (Matthew 5:31-32)?

CONTEXT

Divorce is the third illustration out of six given by Jesus to highlight a new righteousness in the Kingdom of Heaven. It is not a discussion Jesus held at a special time in a designated location. He progressed in His sermon to a contrast between the righteousness of the present Jewish religion (*"righteousness of the scribes and Pharisees"*) to the "righteousness exceeding" (Matthew 5:20).

Jesus' first illustration was "murder" (Matthew 5:21-26). *"Those of old"* limited their discussion to an outward activity of murder, never considering their feelings and emotions, focusing on a stagnant deed. Their righteousness asked, "Did you murder?" The Kingdom's righteousness refused this question because the activity of the deed is not the problem in the Kingdom. The Kingdom asks, "Did you get angry, call him names, have an attitude of contempt, and demean him to the level of a fool?" These questions express a self-centered nature at the core of our being. This self-centeredness is the real issue!

Jesus' second illustration is "morality" (Matthew 5:27-30). "Those of old" limited their discussion to an outward activity, "adultery." Their sexuality was a body drive that needed to be limited to an acceptable standard, the seventh commandment. Their righteousness asked, "Did you commit adultery? Did you lust? Do your eyes see with the perspective of self-centered flesh and the satisfaction of selfish desires? These questions search out a self-centered nature at the core of our being. This self-centeredness is the real issue. This is such a serious issue that Jesus surrounds it with the subject of "hell!"

Now we come to the third illustration, "marriage" (Matthew 5:31-32). He begins this illustration differently. Neither of the previous illustrations begins with a conjunction but the third does, and it is the conjunction "de." This conjunction is ignored by many translations, but our translation (New King James) interprets it to mean *"furthermore."* The primary translation for "de" is the contrasting conjunction "but." Although this may not always be a proper translation, "de" is consistently used as "continuation." In other words, Matthew links this third illustration directly with the second.

In the first illustration, Jesus shifted the issue of murder proposed by *"those of old"* to the inner self-centered motive of anger, and He shifted adultery to the inner self-centered heart in the second illustration. Will this third illustration be any different? In the previous two illustrations, Jesus internalized the issue from outward activity to inner motive. Will he not continue to do so with divorce? The context of this illustration will not allow us to interpret Jesus' statement as instruction for proper divorce proceedings. His discussion does not include the issue of when it is proper to get a divorce.

Jesus calls us to examine our inner heart. Is self-centeredness the determining element of our desires? Will I allow the circumstances of my marriage to reveal the core value of my heart? The pressures I experience, the stress raking my system, and the anxiety I endure are all symptoms of a heart condition. What is that condition? Self-centeredness is the problem; it is verified by the context of our passage.

CONTINUATION

What did Jesus teach about marriage and divorce? He references divorce four times in the Gospels (Matt 5:32; 19:3-9; Mark 10:2-12; Luke 16:18). Jesus' statement in Luke's Gospel is a duplication of our passage from the Sermon on the Mount (Matthew 5:32), and His statement in Mark's Gospel is a duplication of the Pharisees attempts to trap Jesus (Matthew 19:3-9). This means there are only two occasions when Jesus addressed divorce. However, Paul quotes Jesus on this subject in his letter to Corinth (1 Corinthians 7:10-15). No new insight is given to us in this passage.

The remarkable thing in each occasion recorded in the Gospels is Jesus' perspective on the issue being addressed. While the Pharisees highlight divorce, Jesus declares the **"the hardness of your hearts"** (Matthew 19:8). In each instance Jesus is not giving a seminar on divorce, and

He is not trying to settle the debate between the two opposing schools. He calls His disciples to bleed, suffer, and die. This calling applies to the disciples' relationship with other disciples and their link with others.

Matthew records three major events in chapter 19. The first is "marriage and divorce" (Matthew 19:1-12), the second is "mother's and dependents" (Matthew 19:13-15), and the third is "materialism and the depressed" (Matthew 19:16-30). The lesson Jesus teaches in each setting does not seem to address the apparent issue. He called His disciples *"to come after Me, let him deny himself, and take up his cross, and follow Me. For whoever desires to save his life will lose it, but whoever loses his life for My sake will find it"* (Matthew 16:24-25). How does this apply to "marriage and divorce?" How does this apply to "mother's and dependents," those who are less than you are? How does this apply to "materialism and the depressed?"

Because Jesus continually speaks to the destruction of self-centeredness in His teachings, why would He be different in our passage (Matthew 5:32)? Do not approach our passage to find the proper procedure for divorce and remarriage because that is not the focus of Jesus' teaching! We must examine the heart to find any residue of self-centeredness. The fact that we want to argue the issue of marriage and divorce declares the abiding presence of self-centeredness.

CONCLUSION

So what is the conclusion? If we attempt to find solutions to the major social problems of our day, we must look beyond the apparent need. What shall we do about divorce? What is the answer to "same-sex marriages?" How do we solve the crisis of homosexuality? What is the solution to a teenage boy who feels as if he should be a girl? Jesus declares that these things are not the problem! They are symptoms of the problem. We find the problem in the heart filled with self-centeredness. We have not lost our lives to Jesus. It appears even our involvement with Jesus is for our benefit. We continually use Him for what we want. It is time to lose our lives to Him; He wants to use us!

17

KINGDOM MARRIAGE

MATTHEW 5:31-32

"Furthermore it has been said, 'Whoever divorces his wife, let him give her a certificate of divorce.' But I say to you that whoever divorces his wife for any reason except sexual immorality causes her to commit adultery; and whoever marries a woman who is divorced commits adultery" (Matthew 5:31-32).

Jesus is the answer! He is the truth of life! However, this statement leaves most people unmoved because they cannot fathom how He could be the answer. They view the problems and negative circumstances of their world and think the answer is a magical removal of these things however necessary. But Jesus does not use magic. Although we are amazed at His miracles, we continue to live with the obstacles and difficulties that mold and shape our lives. Jesus wants to be the answer to all of our circumstances, but it appears to us that He does nothing about them.

Wait! Jesus really is the answer! But the answer is not in what He does; it is in who He is! It is difficult to explain this to those who have not experienced Jesus. He does not tell you the truth; Jesus is the truth. Truth is not in the data and information He gives you. Truth is in the revelation of who He is in you. We find knowledge and new perspective in intimacy with Him. Our need is not that He remove or change our circumstances, but we need an ever-deepening oneness with Him.

In our studies we call this deepening oneness with Jesus "saturation." Saturation is not a technique or method but a principle of relationship. Will you commit yourself to saturate in the presence of Jesus? Will you develop "a God awareness" in your life, allowing Jesus to invade all aspects of your living? He wants to move from your morning devotions, your prayer before meals, your cry to Him in the moment of crisis to a consistent, moment by moment, interaction between you and Him. What if you relied on Jesus for every involvement of your life, large or small? Instead of figuring out how to source your actions, allow Jesus' mind to be in you.

Allowing Jesus to source your actions will change the focus of your living. Instead of seeking to make it through the day, solving a problem, or achieving a goal, you seek intimacy with Him. Your driving desire becomes Jesus! This new desire will be the one thing you "do." Christianity will cease to be a series of activities and become a relationship with Jesus. You will no longer source your Christian life because He will become your energy. You will saturate in Him!

Saturating in Jesus will change your approach to the Scriptures. The Bible has been a curriculum for specialized students. Many people have made the Bible their roadmap to heaven, an instruction manual for constructing the proper life, or a theological book to support a persuasion. Now the Scriptures become the whispers from the Lover of my soul. As I saturate in His presence, His Word becomes Him speaking to my soul. He takes me beyond the intellectual, academic understanding to the knowledge of His heart. I am no longer studying a book. I am in fellowship with a Person. I saturate in the Living Word by saturating in the Written Word.

My saturation in Jesus is happening in our investigation of the Sermon on the Mount. Our purpose is not to learn data or facts from the passage. We discover Jesus' heart, His tone, and how He thinks. In our previous study, we investigated the concept of our passage (Matthew 5:31-32). This concept is important in life, and we must carefully consider it again. Saturation is not a discovery of facts but a revelation of a concept.

These two verses highlight the subject of marriage and divorce. Many people investigate these verses to reveal the proper procedure for divorce. Arguments arise from the different interpretations of the facts in these verses, causing many questions. What are the grounds for divorce? If I get a divorce, may I remarry? If I marry someone who has been divorced, am I living in adultery? The debates about the answers to these questions continue endlessly. The tragedy of the situation is that we miss the purpose of the passage. Jesus does not answer these questions because they are not the issue He addresses! We do not see or understand it because we did not saturate. Our high intelligence or academic pursuit is not how we understand these verses. Our understanding comes from the presence of Jesus in the context of His Word. The Living Word and the Written Word become real in our lives.

Please allow me to again take you through the concept of Jesus' message in the Sermon on the Mount. Jesus' message (three chapters) shook the world of the disciples. Matthew said that it "knocked them out of their senses," *"the people were astonished at His teaching"* (Matthew 7:28). Jesus was radical from His first word to His last on the Kingdom of Heaven.

Jesus began with a series of "Beatitudes," "The Formation of the Kingdom" (Matthew 5:3-12). His words form congratulations, good fortune, and completeness. This is not something you receive but what you have. The Beatitudes are not a perspective of a heavenly future, but a view of your present state. You do not earn, merit, or achieve this reward because Jesus provides it for you. What all other religions offer as the result of discipline, achievement, and faithfulness, Jesus congratulates you for having now. This state is the Kingdom of Heaven. If you say that you do not live in the Kingdom of Heaven, it is not because it is not yours. Everything associated with the Kingdom is yours. You may refuse to embrace it, but God always provides.

The Kingdom of Heaven is a state of embracing the absolute poverty of your inner spirit (Matthew 5:3). You recognize your helplessness. It is not that you are helpless in mastering certain skills in your physical world, but it is the poverty at the core of your being where your life is sourced. You are to embrace your helplessness as one who "mourns" (Matthew 5:4), like one who lost their dearest loved one. Grief so overtakes your inner being that your life expresses it. Embrace your helplessness with the passion or fervor that affects your perspective on life. If you do, you will be filled with the comfort of Jesus' presence (Matthew 5:4). You will find the Spirit of Jesus merging with your helplessness. When you and Jesus unite, the Kingdom of Heaven is formed. Out of this formation comes all that really matters in life: meekness (Matthew 5:5), inheriting the earth (Matthew 5:5), fulfillment of righteousness (Matthew 5:6), mercy (Matthew 5:7), purity (Matthew 5:8), seeing God (Matthew 5:8), peace (Matthew 5:9), relationship (Matthew 5:9), and intimacy with Him (the Kingdom of Heaven) that rises above all adversities (Matthew 5:10-12). You are not "in" the Kingdom; you have "become" the Kingdom!

Next, Jesus explains the "Function of the Kingdom" (Matthew 5:13-16). How does this Kingdom operate in our world? He uses the imagery of *"salt"* and *"light,"* "being" and "doing." The presence of the Kingdom of Heaven influences your world. What you are in the merger with Jesus transforms everything around you. Your world sees the Father and will stand in awe of Him (Matthew 5:16).

This transformation must have sounded radical to a culture of legalistic religion. The Pharisees developed six hundred and thirteen oral traditions based on the Old Testament. Their righteousness existed in their oral traditions, which they carried out in their temple activities. Their interpretation of the Scriptures demanded this righteousness. Did Jesus propose a new religion? Was He rejecting the Scriptures on which they based their righteousness? Is His proposed Kingdom different from what their promised Messiah would establish?

Jesus answers their question by proclaiming the "Fulfillment of the Kingdom" (Matthew 5:17-48). We have divided it into two sections: "Acknowledgment of the Fulfillment" (Matthew 5:17-20) and "Application of the Fulfillment" (Matthew 5:21-48). Jesus boldly declared His relationship with the Scriptures. He said, **"Do not think"** (nomizo). Do not let the pattern of thinking you have always embraced determine your thoughts now. Twice He said, **"I did not come to destroy."** Our perspective on the Scriptures is so contaminated that Jesus takes us back to what God intended in the Scriptures. The Kingdom of Heaven is what God desires for us and announces in the Scriptures. The Scriptures of the Old Testament find their completion in this new Kingdom relationship.

Jesus' fulfillment of the Kingdom produced a new level of righteousness. The scribes and Pharisees were doing the best they could do. Their source of righteousness was their helplessness. They were self-sourced! Now your helplessness can merge with the righteousness of God! What kind of difference will this make in your life? Even the beginner in this new relationship will far exceed anything self-sourcing can produce (Matthew 5:20).

Jesus knew they did not understand this because they had never experienced it, so He gave them some examples (Matthew 5:21-48). He presented six illustrations. The first one deals with "murder" (Matthew 5:21-26). **"Those of old"** considered their inner helplessness, which was filled with emotional upset, hatred, and bitterness. Anger surfaces when self is challenged. We must not allow these feelings to possess our lives and limit our expressions. The Ten Commandments offered a solution: **"You shall not** *murder.*" This commandment is the best self-sourcing, my helplessness, can exhibit.

The Kingdom of Heaven offers another level of living. If my helplessness can be embraced by God's nature, I can experience a new expression of righteousness. Jesus did not offer a new rule to curb the expression of anger. He proposed an elimination of the anger itself! What if your source of living changes? How will you live if the nature of God were the source of your expression? This change is not "anger management;" this is "anger elimination." It is not a new rule; it is a new Source!

We must see this illustration in light of the idea Jesus proposes. In the "Formation of the Kingdom" (Matthew 5:3-12), we enter into a new state of living. It is a merger between the Spirit of God and our helplessness. This new Kingdom of God will be *"salt"* and *"light"* in our world, the "Function of the Kingdom" (Matthew 5:13-16). It will look like Jesus! He will hang on a cross and cry, "Forgive them!" He will communicate redemption in every encounter. Sin will not survive the atmosphere of this forgiving nature. It will be the "Fulfillment of the Kingdom" (Matthew 5:17-48). Everything God proposed in the Old Testament Scriptures will be completed in this new Kingdom person! It will be a righteousness far exceeding the righteousness of the scribes and Pharisees.

The second illustration is "morality" (Matthew 5:27-30). *"Those of old"* considered their sexuality a body appetite to give pleasure but not abuse. In viewing their helplessness, they saw their core self-centeredness as filled with the desires of the flesh. Lust, uncontrolled urges, and personal satisfaction managed their lives and needed to be limited in its expression. They found the boundary in the Seventh

Commandment of the Ten Commandments, *"You shall not commit adultery."* This limitation was the best they could do sourced by their helplessness, and even this was difficult.

The Kingdom of Heaven offered a new level of righteousness. If my helplessness can be embraced by His Divine nature, a new righteousness can be experienced. Jesus did not offer a new rule to curb the raging desire of the body appetite but proposed a new source for the sexuality of my person. His sourcing will not eliminate my sexual desires but will transform them with a new perspective. The helpless self-centered heart looks through the physical eyes and sees what caters to its desires. What if my helplessness is embraced by His Divine nature? I will have a new perspective! The expression of my sexuality in every area will become the expression of Jesus. The way I walk, the way I dress, the interaction with the opposite gender, and how I view others will all be sourced by this new nature filling my helplessness. Even my sexuality will become *"salt"* and *"light"* in my world. My selfish helplessness will be transformed into a redemptive empowerment.

How will this affect my marriage? OH! "Marriage" is the third example (Matthew 5:31, 32). *"Those of old"* could not endure the normal irritations of marriage. With their helplessness dominated by self-centeredness, they considered benefits only for themselves. When two helpless self-centered people live together the result is conflict. Moses granted using a *"certificate of divorce."* Helpless self-centeredness requires the choice of divorce, and Jesus communicated the one reason for such a provision was our self-centered helplessness (Matthew 19:8).

"Those of old" never questioned the right of divorce. They asked only, "When may we divorce?" They debated the issue of cause, physical circumstance, or justification. The conservative school proposed the only justification for divorce is adultery while the liberal school proposed any unfavorable thing is a basis for divorce. Bad breathe, bad cooking, and finding someone more attractive justified divorce. Self-centered helplessness always looks for the boundary within which to be self-centered. In the emotional anger of life, it is murder; in self-centered sexuality, it is adultery. In marriage, divorce is acceptable, but what is the justifiable cause?

The Kingdom of Heaven offers a new level of righteousness. Jesus does not offer a new rule justifying divorce. Wait! He said, *"for any reason except sexual immorality"* (Matthew 5:32). You must see His statement in light of the second illustration. Sexual immorality is not a matter of physical activity but a matter of the self-centered helplessness of the heart. Because *"all have sinned and fall short of the glory of God"* (Romans 3:23) are we not all guilty of sexual immorality in the self-centered heart? Should we not all hang our heads and cry for deliverance from the self-centeredness of our lives that refuses to embrace our helplessness? Would not embracing and empowering our helplessness by the nature of Jesus enable us in the oneness of marriage?

We must see this illustration in light of the concept Jesus proposes. In the "Formation of the Kingdom" (Matthew 5:3-12), we enter into a new state of living, a merger between the Spirit of God and our helplessness. This new Kingdom of God will be *"salt"* and *"light"* in the world, the "Function of the Kingdom" (Matthew 5:13-16).

It will look like Jesus! Paul said that it would cause me to love my *"wife as Christ also loved the church and gave Himself for her, that He might sanctify and cleanse her"* (Ephesians 5:25, 26). The redemptive nature of Jesus will fill the atmosphere of my home instead of the selfish demand of my desires! Where do we find divorce in that kind of oneness in marriage? This kind of marriage unity will be the "Fulfillment of the Kingdom" (Matthew 5:17-48). Everything God proposed in the Old Testament Scriptures will be completed for the Kingdom person in the marriage! It will be a righteousness far exceeding the righteousness of the scribes and Pharisees. My helplessness cries for His filling!

18

THE MAIN SUBJECT

MATTHEW 5:31-32

"Furthermore it has been said, 'Whoever divorces his wife, let him give her a certificate of divorce.' But I say to you that whoever divorces his wife for any reason except sexual immorality causes her to commit adultery; and whoever marries a woman who is divorced commits adultery" (Matthew 5:31-32).

The context of our passage is of the utmost importance. Over the years people have made assumptions creating issues affecting our understanding. Some of these assumptions come from the Jewish cultural environment of biblical times while the language of the New Testament generates other assumptions. Jesus proposed a new spiritual perception of the Kingdom person, and His proposal also caused assumptions. These assumptions are essential to our understanding of the spiritual concept Jesus relates in our passage.

DESIGN

Jesus' words in our passage are focused on and addressed to men. He follows the biblical idea for the structure of marriage relating directly to the sexuality of the people involved. We could approach this subject from the psychological view and discover important facts, but we are interested in seeing sexuality only through spiritual eyes. God gave male and female different sexuality for creating "one flesh." *"And the Lord God said, 'It is not good that man should be alone; I will make him a helper comparable to him'"* (Genesis 2:18), giving us God's purpose for female sexuality. The English word "complement" best conveys the meaning of this position. The wife is a *"helper"* who "complements" her husband in every way. A helping role does not imply inferiority because the husband also complements his wife.

In these complementary roles, *"the husband is head of the wife"* (Ephesians 5:22). The context of his position is, *"as also Christ is head of the church; and He is the Savior of the body. Therefore, just as the church is subject to Christ, so let the wives be to their own husbands in everything"* (Ephesians 5:23-24). God intended the husband to have a redemptive position with his wife, but his self-centered heart controlled his sexuality. He did not see his leadership position as redemptive, but allowing his selfishness, he dominated his wife for his satisfaction and desires. Self-centeredness is always destructive and never redemptive.

The Jewish culture of Jesus' day was a male dominated society, and the sexuality of man was self-centered. There were no women disciples. Women joined the disciples during the last six months of Jesus' life, providing the financial aid for Jesus (Luke 8:1-3). They were faithful at the cross when the disciples fled in fear. These women met every requirement of a faithful disciple; yet, they were never included in the role. In the Jewish tradition of marriage, the bridegroom had to pay a stipulated price to the bride's father for the privilege of marriage to his daughter. Because the husband paid a price for his wife, this seemed to give him liberty to exercise arbitrary power over her. The husband could renounce or divorce her whenever he chose, but the wife did not have the same privilege. Thus, in our passage (Matthew 5:31-21), Jesus directs His remarks to the self-centered man, not the woman.

DETAIL

Jesus focuses His remarks, clarifying that focus with the statement, *"except for sexual immorality."* Jesus is not talking about the husband who finds his wife unfaithful to him, committing adultery. This is evident when Jesus gives insight by saying, *"causes her to commit adultery; and whoever marries a woman who is divorced commits adultery"* (Matthew 5:32). If the wife has chosen to commit adultery, the reason for the divorce, then the husband's response is not the cause of the adultery.

Therefore, the spiritual truth Jesus communicates does not include the situation where adultery has occurred in marriage. In Jesus' second illustration about "morality," He proposed a description of adultery in the spiritual world. *"Those of old,"* considered adultery only in the physical. There was no provision in the Old Covenant for the cleansing of the self-centered nature that controlled sexuality. The Old Covenant did not have that power. The best *"those of old"* could manage was to put a limit on the expression of their sexuality, *"You shall not commit adultery"* (Matthew 5:27). Jesus moves man to the higher standard of the New Covenant where a man is not to "look" at a woman with lust in his heart. If a person's heart is changed from the nature of self-centeredness to God's nature, what they see and their perspective of others also changes. Under the New Covenant, what adultery is in the physical world, lust is in the spiritual world.

Jesus' third illustration reverts to the Old Covenant view of adultery. In His first two illustrations (murder and morality), Jesus aggressively moves us into the spiritual perspective. He does the same in His discussion of marriage. We have to maintain the spiritual view of the subject being discussed. Jesus uses an interesting combination of words to express this. The statement under consideration is, *"for any reason except sexual immorality."* This phrase is translated from "parektos logos porneia." Our words "porn" and "pornography" come from the Greek word "porneia." Jesus used the word "logos," which on occasion is used as a "cause" or "reason." So what is the idea? "Logos" is the idea or thought being expressed and encourages us to consider the spiritual realm instead of the physical. Jesus' reference is to the idea or thought of sexual immorality.

DONATION

Jesus statement concerns what is "caused" in the woman. He speaks to the husbands and not the wives, desperately concerned about the spiritual view of the issue, the contribution the husband is making to his wife. If the husband's role is spiritual leader, he is to be the redemptive source for his wife. The issue under discussion is "what are you causing in her?"

The Greek word "poieo" is translated *"causes."* The word is used for trees "bearing" (poieo) fruit, referring not just to the action but also to the nature and motive for the action. The nature is driving the expression. Jesus is concerned about the husband, who as spiritual leader is the redemptive force in the home. The husband filled with self-centeredness becomes a manipulative, destructive, damning force in influencing his wife. Jesus is not talking about just the physical act of adultery.

The husband is responsible for creating a state or atmosphere in which the wife is drawn into submission, yielding, and surrendering her life to Christ. The self-centered husband creates a state or atmosphere in which she is drawn to self-centered expression. Instead of pulling her to Christ, he pushes her to a self-centered demonic nature. His self-centered actions cause her to seek to save her life, and instead she loses it. He should be living in the atmosphere of holiness that draws her to lose her life so she will find it. Jesus was concerned about what *"those of old"* were producing in others. The husband who is focused on himself loses perspective of his wife's needs, and he ceases to be the spiritual leader and redeemer in his home. He aids in the production of self-centered sexuality in his wife.

DIVORCE

Now we need a review. Jesus does not speak to the women of His day, but He speaks to the men. The wives did not have the right to divorce; the husbands were the spiritual leaders of the "one flesh" marriage. He set aside any thought of justification for divorce such as the wife involved in adultery. He does not discuss the adulterous wife in this illustration. Jesus' main concern is what the husband is stimulating in the heart of his wife. The husband is to be the spiritual leader responsible for producing an atmosphere in which his wife can surrender to Jesus.

Two Greek words we must examine are paramount to understanding this passage. The Greek word "apostasion" is a legal, technical term for the relinquishing of legal rights. When used in relationship to marriage it means, "divorce." When we hear that someone is "divorced," we know immediately that they were once married but that marriage is no longer binding, and they are now single. No one gets confused or misunderstands using the word "divorce." If a married couple separates but does not legally dissolve the marriage, they are not divorced. The English word "divorce" and the Greek word "apostasion" always mean, a legal dissolution of a marriage.

The Greek word "apostasion" is used only three times in the New Testament. Each time "a certificate of" is used, the word "divorce" is included. This phrase emphasizes the technical and legal aspect of the word's meaning. One of those three uses is in the understanding of *"those of old."* They proposed, *"let him give her a certificate of divorce"* (Matthew 5:31). Moses established this legality, and it has been in effect for hundreds of years (Deuteronomy 24:1).

The second Greek word is "apoluo," a general term used sixty-six times in the New Testament for a variety of situations. It means "releasing, dismissing, sending away (as a crowd or individual), liberating, discharging, releasing from debt, releasing a prisoner, dismissing a servant, forgiving or pardoning a debt or action, releasing from sickness, sending demons from a person, or sending apostles." In the context of our passage it means, "for a husband to send his wife from his house." This is the Greek word equivalent to our English word "separation." "Separation" is never to be confused with "divorce," but is understood as the prelude to divorce, which may or may not occur.

In our passage (Matthew 5:31-32), "apoluo" (separation) is used three times, and "apostasion" (divorce) is used once. The Greek word "apostasion (divorce)" is used in connection with *"it has been said"* (Matthew 5:31). "Apostasion" is not used at all in connection with, *"But I say to you"* (Matthew 5:32). Jesus is NOT discussing the subject of divorce. He is talking about separation! He does not give the biblical grounds for divorce; He does not discuss or describe divorce.

There may be a time to talk about the issue of divorce, but not from this passage. Is divorce applauded and exalted by God in the Scriptures? Absolutely NOT! Jesus is strong on the fact that from the beginning God did not provide for divorce. Divorce was never the intent of His heart. He placed Adam and Eve together in "one flesh" and there was never a provision for divorce. Self-centeredness so possessed the human heart that it destroyed the "one flesh" of marriage. God allowed divorce in such cases. He found it necessary to divorce Israel. *"Then I saw that for all the causes for which backsliding Israel had committed adultery, I had put her away and given her a certificate of divorce; yet her treacherous sister Judah did not fear, but went and played the harlot also"* (Jeremiah 3:8). Is it God's desire and choice? NO! But occasionally it is necessary.

Can a person remarry after being divorced? Perhaps the sin is not in divorce but in remarrying. The intent of God's provision through Moses for divorce was remarriage. After declaring the provision of giving a certificate of divorce (Deuteronomy 24:1), God made the stipulation, *"when she has departed from his house, and goes and becomes another man's wife"* (Deuteronomy 24:2). There is no guidance or condemnation about remarriage in this passage. The provision of divorce was for the possibility of remarriage, which would protect the woman. But these are all issues not discussed in our passage! Jesus addresses none of these issues in the Sermon on the Mount!

What is Jesus' concern? Will you and I embrace our helplessness and allow His person to fill and source us? Will we become dependent instead of independent? Will we recognize the destructiveness of our self-sourcing and discover the full potential in His sourcing (Matthew 5:13-16). We promoted a self-centered, self-sourced, legalistic, religious clique instead of becoming the Kingdom of God fulfilling all the Scriptures (Matthew 5:17-20).

We joined *"those of old"* in trying to manage our anger instead of being delivered from it. We limited the expression of our self-centered wrath and did not commit murder, but in the spiritual world, murder was committed (Matthew 5:21-26). We viewed our sexuality as a body appetite to be controlled by a rule, *"You shall not commit adultery."* All the while in the depth of our being self-centeredness mastered our sexuality and expressed itself in *"lust."* We strut with pride in our walk, demand our rights in relationships, and grab for ourselves in our materialism. We con each other for self-satisfaction, manipulate others for our benefit, and continually parade our joy over the failures of others. Our self-centered sexuality determines our perspective that becomes lust (Matthew 5:27-30).

Our self-centered sexuality appears in our marriages. The old provision was "tired of your wife, divorce her." If you find some unfavorable, unclean thing about her then legally remove yourself from her. Do you see that the real problem is self-centeredness? Jesus speaks to the husbands who are the spiritual leaders of their marriage. Jesus does not discuss divorce or the grounds for divorce. He highlights what happens in the spiritual realm because of self-centeredness. You separated yourself, pushed your wife aside, for your own self-centered desires. Instead of creating a spiritual atmosphere of intimacy and one flesh, drawing her into the fullness of Jesus in her life, you pushed her aside. You left her dangling, emotionally and spiritually deprived of all that would make her the godly wife she could be. She found herself without spiritual leadership and reverted to self-centeredness as you taught her.

Jesus addressed the situation common in His culture. Husbands would easily separate from their wives, leaving these women with no means of support. If they could not return to their father's home, they were homeless. These separated wives' only possibilities were prostitution or another marriage, which created an adulterous situation because they were not legally free from their previous marriage. Why would a husband put his wife in such a situation? The reason is the self-centeredness of his inward heart!

Even though I might be proud that I have never done such to my wife, in the spiritual realm have I lived out of myself, failing in the spiritual leadership of my home? Although my wife has not had an adulterous affair, have I failed to meet her needs emotionally and spiritually, causing her to commit spiritual adultery? Am I not responsible for my "one flesh?" If "she is me" (Genesis 2:23), am I destroying myself when I do not allow Jesus to source me?

19

SPIRITUAL SEPARATION

MATTHEW 5:31-32

"Furthermore it has been said, 'Whoever divorces his wife, let him give her a certificate of divorce.' But I say to you that whoever divorces his wife for any reason except sexual immorality causes her to commit adultery; and whoever marries a woman who is divorced commits adultery" (Matthew 5:31-32).

There are people who are spiritually sensitive and desire the presence of God in their lives. We know what it feels like to live in the violation of His will, and this rests heavily on us because we are guilty. We understand that the violation of His will in our lives destroys our relationship with God. The only chance for any peace in His presence is forgiveness. The forgiving heart of God is the theme of the Scriptures. Jesus said, *"Therefore I say to you, every sin and blasphemy will be forgiven men"* (Matthew 12:31). We can draw assurance from John when he wrote, *"If we confess our sins, He is faithful and just to forgive us our sins and to cleanse us from all unrighteousness"* (1 John 1:9).

Jesus is *"the image of the invisible God"* (Colossians 1:15). Jesus' characteristics, as highlighted in the Gospel accounts, reveal the mind and nature of God. Jesus always forgives, even in the worst of circumstances. Enduring the suffering of the cross, He said, *"Father, forgive them"* (Luke 23:34). Amid a pressing crowd, Jesus said to the paralytic lowered in front of Him, *"Son, be of good cheer; your sins are forgiven you"* (Matthew 9:2). The only thing Jesus will not tolerate is a self-centered rebellious attitude that will not embrace forgiveness.

Although I have never been divorced, it seems to me that the difficulty is forgiveness. I can imagine it would be a struggle to forgive the spouse who repeatedly injured the offering of your heart, but it may be an even greater hurdle to forgive yourself for your part in the destruction of your marriage. We are often haunted by our failure in the context of our relationships. Is divorce like the death of a spouse, only they never go away? How do you forgive yourself and the others involved to move on?

It is not my intention to increase guilt regarding divorce. Whatever your situation, this is a call to learn the spiritual lessons for which God allowed this to happen. Was my divorce right or wrong? Divorce is never right! We recognize the cause of every divorce is the heart of sin, which is self-centeredness. You must allow what happened to cause your surrender to Jesus and never again allow self-sourcing in your life!

Our study of this passage leads us to discover that Jesus is not addressing the issue of divorce. Although most translations interpret this passage with Jesus using the word "divorce" three times, I oppose these interpretations. The Greek word "apostasion" is a legal, technical term for the relinquishing of legal rights. When used in relation to marriage, it means "divorce." When we hear that someone is "divorced," we understand they were once married but that marriage is no longer binding, and the people are now single. The word "divorce" and "apostasion" always mean a legal dissolving of marriage. The word "apostasion" is used only once in our passage and refers to "a certificate of divorce." The Greek word "apoluo" is a general term used sixty-six times in the New Testament for a variety of situations. This is the Greek word equivalent to our English word "separation." "Separation" as applied to marriage is never confused with "divorce." We understand that a "separation" is often a prelude to a "divorce," which may or may not occur. Jesus is NOT talking about the subject of divorce but about the subject of separation! He does not give biblical grounds for divorce. He does not describe a state of adultery for those who remarry after divorce. He is not talking about divorce at all. Every time *"divorce"* appears in these two verses except for *"a certificate of divorce,"* the word should have been translated "separates."

In the Sermon on the Mount, Jesus continually exposes the self-centered heart. These two verses are a continuation of His theme. The scribes and Pharisees separated from their wives at the slightest upset, and according to Jewish law they should have given her a certificate of divorce. However, the sexuality of the husband dominated by self-centeredness would separate from his wife and not bother with the certificate of divorce. Separation without divorce meant the marriage was not dissolved. The woman was left helpless without support, forcing her into adultery, either prostitution or remarriage even though she was still legally married. The problem was not in the legal divorce but in the separation.

Jesus does not speak to the *"woman"* but forcefully exposes the self-centered husband. The Bible defines the role of the husband as *"head of the wife"* (Ephesians 5:23). The self-centered heart hears those words and interprets them as "boss, use, and manipulate," but that was never the spiritual intent. Paul clearly speaks to this in his letter to the Ephesians. *"Husbands, love your wives, just as Christ also loved the church and gave Himself for her, that He might sanctify and cleanse her with the washing of water by the word, that He might present her to Himself a glorious church, not having spot or wrinkle or any such thing, but that she should be holy and without blemish"* (Ephesians 5:25-28). The biblical role of the husband is a spiritual role!

My responsibility as a husband is to provide an atmosphere in which my wife can flourish spiritually in intimacy and oneness with Jesus. I am to protect her from every evil power and influence that would drag her into self-centeredness. Marriage is the commitment of death to self-centeredness. I am giving myself to my wife in a spiritual, physical, and legal sense, losing my life to my wife. Loving my wife in this manner is the principle of the Kingdom that Jesus expressed when He said, *"For whoever desires to save his life will lose it, but whoever loses his life for My sake will find it"* (Matthew 16:25). When I lose my life to my wife and seek only to meet her needs, my needs are met! When I use her to meet my needs, neither her needs nor mine are met.

Jesus talks about the problem of self-centeredness in our passage. The new righteousness of the Kingdom that exceeds the righteousness of the scribes and Pharisees is a righteousness of death to self-centeredness. In the self-centeredness of the old righteousness, the man separated from his wife in the marriage relationship, instead of giving her a certificate of divorce. He did not legally divorce but mentally and spiritually separated from his wife, most often dismissing her from his home. Even if he allowed her to remain in his home his, self-centeredness produced an atmosphere that left her alone and without support, and in each situation he was not following the biblical principle of marriage.

SECURITY

Understanding the culture of Jesus' day is of utmost importance. The culture was a male dominated society; the woman was slightly above the category of slave. The bridegroom paid a fee to the father of the bride for the privilege of marriage to her. The self-centered male developed an attitude of ownership of his wife. Only the husband had the right to divorce. The woman had no means of support outside marriage. Her security was in her husband. With this attitude the debate focused on the "grounds for divorce." If the wife committed adultery, the husband was obviously justified in giving her a certificate of divorce. However, the husband could commit adultery, but the wife was without the same option.

The School of Shammai taught that physical adultery was the only grounds for divorce. The School of Hillel disagreed with that position, and they gave a liberal interpretation of the statement *"some uncleanness in her"* (Deuteronomy 24:1). Her "uncleanness" could include burning his food or merely over salting it. If the husband saw another woman whose appearance pleased him more than his wife's, divorce was acceptable. In this atmosphere the woman lived in a state of physical insecurity.

We have been looking at the physical security of the wife in Jesus' day. What about the emotional and spiritual security of her life? In female sexuality God placed the need for security and stability in intimacy. Although the physical provisions of life contribute to her security, they are not the final answer. In illustrating the righteousness exceeding the righteousness of the scribes and Pharisees (Matthew 5:20), Jesus moved from a physical accomplishment to the spiritual realm. A person cannot murder in the physical realm and be righteous (Matthew 5:21). However, anger in the spiritual realm is spiritual murder (Matthew 5:22). The focus of male sexuality was reduced to a body drive. Therefore, abstaining from adultery accomplished righteousness in the physical (Matthew 5:27). But Jesus explained that our hearts determine our sexuality, how we see things (Matthew 5:28). Our core selfishness in the spiritual realm is equal to the act of adultery in the physical. This same principle was applied to Jesus' view of marriage. Remember, He is not discussing divorce in our passage. In the spiritual realm, masculine sexuality lives for itself and deprives feminine sexuality of spiritual and emotional security. She no longer experiences the purpose of her creation, *"bone of my bones and flesh of my flesh"* (Genesis 2:23). The husband ceases to embrace the wife with the security of "she is me!"

The self-centered husband can neglect his role as the figure of Christ to his wife in the spiritual realm. He might feel justified that he has not physically divorced her or separated her from his home, but instead of enveloping her in stability, intimacy, and security he uses and abuses her for his physical satisfaction. When Jesus discussed this attitude with His disciples, their response was astounding! *"If such is the case of the man with his wife, it is better not to marry"* (Matthew 19:10). They thought if you cannot use your wife for your benefit, why would you want to marry? To the self-centered heart, marriage is beneficial only when my needs are met.

Jesus was speaking to the masculine sexuality of His day. The role of the husband in the Kingdom was to provide an atmosphere of security in which his wife could experience spiritual intimacy with Jesus. The husband is the "Christ-figure" to his wife. This was the failure of the first sin (Genesis 3). Adam failed to provide the spiritual leadership in his home. Eve played the role of spiritual leader and sin was born. Sin appeared in a conversation between Eve and the serpent. Adam refused to take part in this spiritual discussion. When God came walking in the garden, He was looking for Adam (Genesis 3:9). Although Eve experienced the consequences of sin with all creation, it was Adam that God confronted first! He failed to give spiritual security in his home.

STABILITY

Providing "stability" for his wife is another aspect of the spiritual atmosphere of the husband, the key to security. There is no security unless stability is present. Security comes with consistency. A variety of men came to Jesus with good intentions of discipleship. They were captivated by His message and miracles. Jesus radically called them to consistency. He said to one person, *"No one, having put his hand to the plow, and looking back, is fit for the kingdom of God"* (Luke 9:62).

Jesus is not discussing divorce in our passage (Matthew 5:31-32). He highlights the "separation" happening in the marriages of His culture. The problem with the marriages was not divorce but separation without a certificate of divorce. Jesus sees the problem not just as a physical separation, leaving the wife with no support, but separation in the spiritual realm. The physical separation was possible only because of the spiritual separation that preceded it. The physical separation and divorce is a product of spiritual separation. The role of the husband is to provide security that is possible only because of consistency in the spiritual atmosphere of the marriage.

In Jesus' culture, self-centered masculinity produced an atmosphere of instability. The wife did not know what her husband might do next. If the physical standard was do not murder (Matthew 5:21), he was free to vent emotionally in the home to express his upset. The husband determined the quality of the day and the atmosphere of the home, and there were days when everything was wonderful, but other days were filled with anger. When the circumstances of his life outside of his home caused his emotional upset and he could not vent on the people there, he then chose to lash out at home. The husband was responsible for the stability of the spiritual atmosphere of his home. This stability provided a security in which his wife could grow.

If the physical standard was do not commit adultery (Matthew 5:27), the husband was free to engage in lust, flirtations, and emotional affairs. His wife was not the focus of his love; one flesh marriage became dissolved in self-centered desires and activities. The emotional and romantic security of the wife was destroyed, and stability was not present.

Security and stability are impossible to maintain because we have up-and-down experiences. How may we not be affected by our world and our circumstances? That is Jesus' premise in the Sermon on the Mount. He calls us to embrace our helplessness (Matthew 5:3). He will come in His fullness and source our lives. We become the Kingdom in our home. Self-centeredness can never produce security or stability. The atmosphere in which the wife can grow and find spiritual maturity in Jesus is destroyed by the self-centeredness of the husband.

SPIRITUALITY

The husband cannot save his wife. Jesus is our Savior. However, if the intent of every Christian is to be the light of the world and the salt of the Earth that displays good works and glorifies our Father in heaven (Matthew 5:13-16), how much more must this happen in our homes? This mandate is the responsibility of the husband for his wife. The spiritual atmosphere of the home is the responsibility of the husband. He is to create a home where his wife can experience spiritual growth in Jesus, without obstacles.

Jesus calls us to the marriage of the New Covenant. Losing our lives to each other is the chief ingredient. We are to embrace our helplessness in the mourning manner that allows the Spirit of Jesus to source us. Meekness, fullness, mercy, purity, seeing God, peace and rejoicing amid of adversity will flow from this (Matthew 5:3-12), which does not produce separation but intimacy with each other and Jesus.

Made in the USA
Middletown, DE
27 August 2020